M000233448

MAD FOR JESUS

Mad for Jesus

The Vision of the
World Wide Message Tribe

Andy Hawthorne with Craig Borlase

Hodder & Stoughton
LONDON SYDNEY AUCKLAND

British Library Cataloguing in Publication Data

A record for this book is available from the British Library

ISBN 0 340 74563 0

Typeset by Hewer Text Ltd, Edinburgh
Printed and bound in Great Britain by
Clays Ltd, St Ives plc

Hodder and Stoughton
A Division of Hodder Headline Ltd
338 Euston Road
London NW1 3BH

To my best friends Michele, Sam and Beth.
You know what, I love you all very much!

Contents

Acknowledgments

Very special thanks to Craig Borlase, first of all for being a top bloke and secondly for spending hours sorting out my rather dodgy manuscript. To Richard Johnson and all the noble trustees of the Message, plus respect to all the wonderful Message full-time staff, Rob Johnson and all the office team, Rob Ruston and all the truly humble operations team, all Eden workers and not forgetting of course Mark Pennells and Zarc Porter. There would not be a Message to Schools or World Wide Message Tribe without you lovely men and women and I know it.

Also to all the faithful supporters of the Message over the last few years who have stood with us in our dream to see Manchester thoroughly blitzed with the good news.

Introduction: Barefoot in India

In 1883 Captain Robert Hawthorne bought a one-way ticket to India. He wasn't on the run and he wasn't going to fight (at least not with guns). He was a Salvation Army missionary pioneer, and he was my great-grandfather.

He had plenty to think about during the three-month voyage; as one of the first Salvation Army missionaries to visit the country the task that faced him and his two colleagues was immense. Still, he was pretty fired up about it, partly as before he had left, William Booth, the founder of the Salvation Army, urged him to 'get inside their skins'.

Robert had something else to think about. During their leaving ceremony in London, a beautiful young Salvation Army officer stood up and sang a solo. Robert had never seen her before, but in a burst of either cocky arrogance or prophetic holiness, he turned to his two travelling companions and told them that she was the girl he was going to marry. When she became a missionary in India a few years later, they met again, fell in love and got married. Over 100 years later there are a few more of us Hawthornes around.

When Robert and his co-workers got to India, it wasn't long before they realised that their Salvation Army uniforms were a little out of place. Back in London they were something to be proud of, but in India they reminded the natives of the uniforms worn by the British soldiers who had colonised their country. The Englishmen decided to ditch their precious threads and instead started wearing traditional Indian costume. Gradually they absorbed more influences from the culture that surrounded them: the housing, the food and the customs, even to the point of not wearing any shoes.

Giving up your shoes might not sound like one of the most radical acts around, but when I read a book about Robert and his mates, I realised that it had a big effect on their lives. One of his colleagues wrote this: 'Even when tramping along on a burning road with sharp stones and thorns like darning needles sticking into you, I look up and not down, and the pain and the dreariness go away and I am happy, supremely happy.'

That supreme happiness came from the two things that make life worth living: an intimate and personal relationship with Jesus and a burning desire to share this Jesus with others. Apparently, the young Salvation Army pioneers competed with each other with new ideas and plans to win people over for Christ. Bit by bit they took on more and more of the culture in order to 'become all things to all men to win a few', and it wasn't long before Captain Hawthorne became known as 'Jaibhai' – taking on an Indian name in order to bring people to Christ.

I believe that there is a new breed of missionary

pioneers being born in Britain right now. People may not be spending three months on a boat to reach the ends of the earth, but they are going a few miles down the road. Like the Salvation Army pioneers, though, they are taking a one-way ticket into the toughest places: the inner cities. William Booth encouraged his workers to 'walk back across the bridges', to go against the tide and find the people who needed Jesus the most. There is so much life in the churches of Britain today, so many things to get excited about, but sadly that life is only reaching a tiny fraction of the population. It can't be right that over 65 per cent of the population in this country are considered working class, and yet less than 1 per cent of the church are working class, and it can't be right that in Manchester, our city, my city, 80 per cent of the Christians live in the suburbs alongside 20 per cent of the people, while only 20 per cent of the Christians live in the urban areas next to 80 per cent of the people. What is even more upsetting is that many of those few Christians who do live in the urban areas actually commute out to the suburban churches for their Sunday and mid-week services. No wonder the devil is having a field day in the inner city.

You might have guessed that this book isn't just the story of the World Wide Message Tribe (but we will have some of that later, and hopefully there will be some lessons to learn from it). It's certainly not the autobiography of me, a 39-year-old evangelist who feels like he's just getting started. What it is, though, is much more simple: it's a story of a growing group of people who are running with a vision to see Manchester radically changed.

Let's face it, Manchester – the city and the surrounding Greater Manchester area – is long overdue for bit of change. Many evangelistic organisations describe it as 'one of the hardest places to do a mission in the world', and for years the situation has gone unchecked. As in any major population centre, there are many social and economic problems that face residents. Crime, unemployment and the breakdown of the family are all instantly recognisable, and housing policies of transferring inner-city communities to out of town estates have only made things worse. The church has also faced its own problems, as factions and back-stabbing have sprung up and unity is shunned.

While the social problems are taking longer to sort out, the church has lately been going through something of a turnaround. In 1993 Frank Green, a local minister, was praying with his wife, Deborah, about the situation. In 1992 they had been involved in running the city's first March for Jesus. It had been a big success, especially by Manchester's standards, but when they tried to carry it on the following year any previous enthusiasm seemed to have fizzled out. In answer to their frustrated prayers, Frank had an impression of a walled city whose defences had been all but destroyed by continual attack. There were a few strong towers left surrounding the city, and as he watched, he saw new walls spring up between them. As the defences were once again able to resist the enemy, new towers were able to be built inside the city. To Frank and Deborah this immediately made them think of Manchester: if the strong towers were the churches, then walls had to be unity. The inner city was a spiritual wasteland, but it gave them hope that if the churches could unite, then the whole landscape could change. That October they set up Prayer Network and invited all denominations to take part. Six years later it attracts about 700 people each quarter and is widely considered to be one of the most exciting prayer movements in the country.

Eleven years ago we started trying to put on city-wide missions, getting the churches of Manchester on board for something called 'The Message '88'. It was at this time that God really spoke to us from the book of Isaiah, chapter 43. These were the verses that really stood out:

> See, I am doing a new thing! Now it springs
> up; do you not perceive it? I am making a way
> in the desert and streams in wasteland. The
> wild animals honour me, the jackals and the
> owls, because I provide water in the desert and
> streams in the wasteland, to give drink to my
> people, my chosen, the people I formed for
> myself that they may proclaim my praise.

From those early days onwards God has been telling us that we should aim for the toughest places. The result is that we have concentrated on Manchester, a city that's never seen revival, and one that to so many evangelistic organisations is a spiritual wasteland. We have known that we should concentrate on young people, as they are the biggest problem the church in Britain has got: we just can't hold on to them. If we could only get them to stay in the church once they've started coming, then the church would start to grow again, and we would be taking this nation for Jesus. We know that our target is not just Manchester's nice young people, but those rough ones from the inner city. The wasteland and the desert have been our fields, and this book shows how the vision for them has grown, how it has changed us, and how we want to see this city turned around.

This isn't just nice a idea to keep us from getting bored. We are a bunch of people with a vision that God has confirmed time and time again: that Manchester is going to be changed. We believe this change will happen not only through the Tribe, Message 2000 and the work of Eden, but also through the many other good things that are springing up all over this city. These different components are all part of God's eye, looking down on Manchester right now.

1

Catching the Bug

Fortunately God's work isn't limited to barefoot mad-for-Jesus missionaries in India. He is working all over the world, and at some point in 1960 he was at work in Hambleton Road, Cheadle, saving a housewife called Christine Hawthorne, my mum.

I was only four months old so my memory's a bit of a blank, but my mum tells me that she was so excited about her new faith that she did everything possible to tell my dad about Jesus. He was a streetwise journalist who thought he knew the score about most things and didn't really have much time for Jesus. My mum used to leave tracts lying about the house, and would turn virtually every conversation they had around to Jesus. Even the boiling time of a pan of carrots managed to become a illustration of how God wanted to soften his heart. But all it did was drive a wedge between her and Dad.

My mum's conversion was part of a mini-revival that was going on in the street. There had been five or six families who had been saved over a very short period of time, and Bible studies were springing up all the way down the road. Most of this had been sparked off by the work and prayers of a wonderful old lady called

Olive Clarke. She's a total saint, and through her there were plenty of housewives who had met with Jesus and were now praying for their husbands.

After about three months of carrot analogies and tracts in the bathroom, a confirmation class started up at the local church. To Mum's astonishment, Dad expressed an interest in going. Halfway through one of the last classes – having argued his way through all the others – he sat down and talked to the curate, Tony Turner. Tony gave him some cheesy analogy about how you never know that a chair is going to hold you up unless you sit on it. He told him that unless he put his faith in God, he would never know if God was able to save him. My dad, worldly-wise hack that he was, was gobsmacked by this little analogy. When they went home he told Mum that he wanted to become a Christian. They knelt down by the bed and Dad gave his life to the Lord. Mum says she remembers praying passionately at that time that their three children – myself, Simon and Michael – would all come to know Jesus as well. Despite it looking a bit dodgy at times, God has answered her prayer in full.

Michael was always a bit of a good lad, doing well at school and going on to become head of English at a big school in Shropshire. Simon and I, however, took a different route. We went to church until we had a choice not to, preferring teenage rebellion over boring church. Simon became a bit of a punk, having purple hair and being the first lad I knew in the 70s to have an earring. He got into things in a big way: from drugs to trouble with the police. I wasn't too much of an angel either, and I remember my headmaster telling me at the end of year eleven that if I ever turned up at school again I would be trespassing. I don't think anyone was very surprised when I didn't stay on for the sixth form. Instead I went and got a job as a cabinetmaker, simply because the only qualification I got from school was one O-level in woodwork. I had wasted my education, despite the fact that when I was twelve I had made a commitment to Jesus at a concert by a Christian band called 'The Sheep'.

The Sheep were an American band who used to play rock and roll covers of songs like 'O happy day'. It sounds terrible now but I remember thinking they were pretty good. At the end of the gig an evangelist spoke and invited those of us who wanted to accept Jesus and go to heaven to bow our heads and join in with a prayer. It seemed like a fair offer to me, so I got my head down and listened as this American evangelist geezer stood behind me, shouting, 'Hallelujah! Praise the Lord, you've given your life to Jesus.' I didn't feel that different at the time, but it got me going along to church for a few months. It didn't take long for my enthusiasm to wear off, especially when being a Christian began to seem like such hard work. There were too many things going on in my life that took me further away from God, and after six months I had stopped going to church altogether. It was rebellion time.

Shortly after I had left school my parents moved to Wales, leaving me behind in Cheadle. I was sixteen, with my own place to live and a personal aim to lose the plot as much as possible. I tried absolutely everything, living the high life with what seemed like quite a decent wage I was bringing home as a cabinetmaker. I was convinced that I was having a good time, but God was on my case and he was answering Mum and Dad's prayers that had had them on their knees for years.

As well as praying hard for us, my mum tried her hand at a bit of practical evangelism, buying us a Christian book each year as one of our Christmas presents. As dutiful non-Christian sons we always ignored them, stuffing them under our beds or using them as firelighters. She always prayed that God would use the books to get through to us, and one year it paid off.

My brother Simon was going out with a girl called Lesley. One day she was looking around a second-hand bookshop when she saw a copy of a book called *Turned on to Jesus* by Arthur Blessett. Because a friend had been telling her about Jesus she paid the five pence required and took it home to read. She was so impressed with it that she gave it to Simon for him to read. He opened the book and inside the front cover were the words 'To Simon, with love from Mum, Christmas 1972'. He recognised Mum's handwriting and immediately knew that this was the book Mum had bought him a few Christmases before. Even now no one is sure how the book got from his bedroom to the second-hand bookshop, but the whole thing had the mark of God all over it. It is just like the hound of heaven to go after Simon and not let him go. When Lesley gave him the book he soon began to realise that as well as being 'with love from Mum', it was also 'with love from God'. He read it with a passion, and just a few days later, while he was driving in his Bedford van, he gave his life to Jesus, saying that same prayer that Dad had said seventeen years earlier.

The Holy Spirit took over and Simon wept like a

little baby. The next time I saw him I knew he was a different man: the purple hair and dreaded earring were still in place, but he was different. He was telling his friends and me that Jesus had completely changed his life and set him on fire. I was seventeen years old and wanted to be a bit of a lad, so this kind of chat wasn't quite the sort of thing I was after, but he just kept on talking. I eventually gave in and agreed to go to church with him. It wasn't a particularly amazing service that we went to, but I remember coming out and thinking that it was a good thing I had just done. For the next six months I was pubbing and clubbing it in Manchester five or six nights and spending one night at church each week. Every time I went along I left feeling good about it until one Sunday evening Simon gave his testimony. He told the congregation exactly how he'd become a Christian and went through all the things that God had done for him. That night my heart melted, and I knew that I wanted it. I wanted to experience the same change that had happened to my brother, to get in touch with the power of Jesus. I went home and knelt by my bed. I can remember saying, 'God, I don't know if you're prepared to have me, but if you are I'm really going to go for it. I'm not going to stuff it up like I did when I was twelve.' I wanted this to be different to what had happened after that Sheep concert. Whatever it cost, I was up for it.

I'd never really heard the parable of the prodigal son about how God welcomes people back, but in my bedroom I sensed that God was having me back and setting me on fire. I woke up the next morning feeling like I wanted to talk to people about Jesus, feeling like

I wanted to read the Bible. I didn't speak in tongues but I believe God filled me with his Spirit and gave me the gift and the heart of an evangelist. In many ways it is precisely that which has kept me going these last twenty years of being a Christian: a passion for seeing people who don't know Jesus find him for themselves. Once I'd got up from beside my bed, Simon and I spent the next few months going around the pubs in Cheadle telling everybody we knew about Jesus, and spending ages each day reading the Bible and praying. We were so fired up for Jesus that our lives had undergone a massive change.

Shortly after I became a Christian my mum and I went to the Keswick Bible Convention. I was blown away by this massive throng of five thousand Christians all meeting under a huge banner that read 'All One in Christ Jesus'. After one of these meetings my mum introduced me to an old lady whose name was Olive Clarke.

'Ah,' she said. 'So you're Andrew. I've been praying for you every week for the past seventeen years. Do you know Jesus?'

Stunned, I told her that I did.

'And your brothers, Simon and Michael, I've been praying for them too. Do they know Jesus?'

Even more stunned I told her that, yes, Jesus had turned them both around. I told Olive that one by one all of us Hawthorne boys had become Christians and that God was blessing the family so much. She was blown away too, and I'll never forget her telling me about how she had prayed for her own father every day of her Christian life. It wasn't until he was eighty-seven years old that the stubborn old thing finally became a Christian himself.

When you get to heaven, you will notice a gigantic mansion with an immense garden. That will be the home of Mrs Olive Clarke, the wonderful saint. That lady's faithful prayers are the reason that I am a Christian, despite the fact she had never met me. I am also sure that God loves to work in family units; he hears our prayers for our family and stores them up; he knows how we feel about our mums and dads, brothers and sisters who aren't Christians. Right through the Bible God loves to save entire families and tribes. Even if they don't respond till they are on their death bed, it is worth praying those prayers, crying out to God to save the people we love the most. It seems clear to me that one of the great joys of getting into heaven is going to be the surprise of seeing the different people who were saved at the eleventh hour. I remember talking to Eric Delve – who is now a vicar – and he told me that he had never been with anybody on their deathbed who wasn't ready to pray the sinner's prayer and ask Jesus into their lives. It's my guess that there will be many of our families with us for all eternity who don't deserve to be there, who haven't lived for Jesus, but who are there by the grace of God. Surely it is worth our while praying those prayers even when it seems like a lost cause?

When I became a Christian, Cheadle was in the middle of the closest thing to revival that anyone there had ever seen. The local youth group started growing at an outrageous rate, going from being just a handful of young people to the largest Church of England youth group in Britain. It took just over a year for the numbers to reach a couple of hundred, and by that time a much needed new curate had arrived. Wally Ben is now an esteemed bishop, but back then he had absolutely no experience of youthwork and felt completely out of his depth. He decided to do the only sensible thing, and spent a day each week locked away in his flat in Didsbury. Thankfully he wasn't hiding, but praying that God would do something. He pleaded with God to show him how to lead this mass of new Christians, and God took notice.

At that time my brother had joined a Christian punk rock band – the Bill Mason Band. They and others started going around local schools, helping to bring in all these fresh Christians. It was fantastic, and it was probably at that time that I caught the bug for schools work myself. It was obvious that there was a massive mission field on our own doorstep.

In the schools and colleges of Manchester an increasingly pagan generation were growing up without any real understanding of even the most basic elements of Christianity. It's got to be said that as a nation we have forgotten about God for the last fifty years since World War II. It's payback time now, and the price is rising levels of family breakdown, crime, suicide and many other social problems. What could be more rewarding and exciting than committing your life to changing this situation? By working and praying towards individuals being brought back to God, by expecting to be part of a whole nation's return to the Creator, you are signing up for the most rewarding and dangerous work out there.

These were some of the basics that we learnt back then. When we started to think, talk and pray about the church, it became clear that as an institution, the church has failed to understand what it is there for. The main purpose is not to be a cosy club for the few who have jumped through enough hoops and learnt enough of the jargon to call it home; the church is for out there. The church is meant to be what C. T. Studd called a 'rescue shop', going to a hurting world with the unimaginably good news of Jesus. What's more, the church needs to make sure that the way it communicates makes sense to the people it tries to reach. Accessibility and interaction should be a total priority of every Bible-believing church. Of course, at the very top of our agenda needs to be the issue of how we stay faithful to the age-old truths of Christianity, but our methods of sharing those truths with others should be a close second. So how do we do it? No matter how great the coming revival is, it's fairly unlikely that people are going to come knocking on our church doors saying, 'What must I do to be saved?' We have to go out there in the power of the Holy Spirit, just like Peter and the boys did way back in the years of bread and sandals, and in the same way that radical believers have been doing ever since.

If we are really called to go where the people are, what better place to go to than the schools? It has amazed us all how open the schools are to us going in and working with their pupils. It even seems to be getting easier, just as long as you aren't a dribbling fanatic who tries to raise the dead in assemblies and have appeals just before double maths. The doors are wide open, and rightly so. We Christians should be allowed to go and teach what the Bible says and explain to people what the world's biggest religion is all about. I believe that many more Christians should be praying and trying to get into their local schools to help them teach about Jesus Christ. After all, he is the central figure of human history, and the Bible is the most amazing book ever written. What's the point of having religious education if we haven't got the believers to teach it? These are the arguments that the Tribe have used for the last seven years, and it's the same bug I caught in 1978, as a fresh-faced 18-year-old excuse for an evangelist.

Pleasure and Pain

I'm worried that I might be looking at the past through rose-tinted spectacles, but as I think about those early years of being a Christian, all I can remember is a time of total blessing. As if meeting Jesus wasn't enough, I also had my eye on Michele Jones, a hot-looking 15-year-old who had become a Christian at one of my brother's gigs with the Bill Mason Band. Despite the fact that I was the 18-year-old youth leader I knew I had to get in there, and sure enough I did. She became the love of my life and we married five years later.

More good things were happening for me at work. While it meant quitting the first job that I had ever really enjoyed – selling melamine-faced chipboard for kitchens – I started working with Simon in the business that he'd set up a year earlier. We sold leather crafts, fashion belts and all that kind of stuff. It also meant that I had loads of opportunities to be doing bits of evangelism on the side.

Several opportunities came my way during those years for me to go into full-time Christian work. At one point I even thought about becoming an Anglican vicar, but it never fell into place so I carried on working with Simon. We were working hard at building up the business, and over time we moved out of the leather crafts market (hand-stitched tool-belts never did seem that cool), and into the world of fashion. We might not have had offices in Paris, Milan or London (Longsight Industrial Estate was more our style), but we were doing pretty well selling to high-street stores. Back then all the staff were Christians, and each day kicked off with a prayer time on the factory floor. As things got bigger we ran out of Christians and thought it might be a good thing if we took a few lads on from the job centre. The daily prayer meetings carried on the same, although this time there were a few blokes staring around, worrying that they had ended up in an asylum.

In the early 1980s Lady Diana arrived on the scene and set off a series of chain reactions that affected the whole nation. It seemed that whatever she wore became an instant hit and, because she was into accessories at the time, that was good news for businesses like ours. I don't remember exactly how it happened, but she might have gone out one night wearing a pair of men's braces. By the following Monday morning just about every young girl in Britain had to have their own pair of Lady Di braces. We had one little machine to make them, and soon found ourselves with orders for almost a million pairs.

We were desperate for help, so we went back to the job centre to see what they could do. We managed to get hold of a few more machines, and by the next day we were opening our doors to the biggest bunch of reprobates we had ever seen. We had no idea what a recruitment policy was, and the job centre had taken us at our word when we told them to send anybody who was prepared to work hard. What we got were all the lads who had just come out of Strangeways Prison or who had got sacked by every other employer in the area. There were some real nutters among them, and they brought with them all kinds of problems; from graffiti and vandalism to violence and theft. But what really bothered me and Simon was not just that they were wrecking our factory and not making a lot of braces, but that as we got to know them it became obvious the lads knew absolutely nothing about Jesus. In that respect they probably weren't much different from most young people in Britain today; and they literally were pagans. They had no understanding of the cross, the resurrection or the need for a personal relationship with Jesus. For them Jesus was just another way of swearing.

One day Simon and I were sat at the 1987 Harrogate Fashion Fair trying to work out how we could present our faith to them. We were talking about how hopeless the church was at trying to reach this kind of guy with the gospel. We spent all afternoon coming up with increasingly crazy ideas. Eventually we got to the point of imagining someone getting all the churches in Manchester to work together in supporting an event that would reach the city's toughest areas. It would need to be something pretty big, so we guessed that we'd have to take over the most credible rock venue in the area, which at that time was the three-thousand-capacity Apollo Theatre. Because we were in that kind of mood we decided that it would be too dull just to book it for one night, so instead we reckoned that it would be best if we had it for a whole week.

We were on a roll, and chatted for ages about how fantastic it would be if we could stuff that week full of credible evangelism that made sense to teenagers. We weren't talking about the normal cringe-making stuff that the church put on, but a series of events of such quality that thousands of people would be blown away. We spent all afternoon working on these dreams, and towards the end it felt as if God's finger was pointing down at us, encouraging us to have a go. It didn't take long for these 'what if?' suggestions to become 'why not?' decisions. We decided to go ahead and book the venue as well as to write to all the churches in Manchester to try to get them behind us. Later that day as we drove home it felt as though my car was floating six inches above the road. I felt so excited; I was sure that God had spoken, and that despite the fact I was an unknown youth group evangelist who made braces, my brother and I were about to do something mad for him.

I went home that night and spoke to my long-time confidant and friend, Val Grieve. When I had finished telling him of the plans he suggested that I went round to see him the next day. I sat in bed that night and opened my Bible, ready to tackle that day's reading from my *Bible in One Year*. I was up to Isaiah 43, and before I read it I asked God if our plan was from him, to give me some sort of encouragement from the Bible over the next days. Looking back I wish I had had the bottle to ask him to speak to me right then, but God knew what he was doing. I believe that out of all the verses in the Bible, those found in Isaiah 43 were the very best ones that I could have read that night. As I started reading them they seemed to jump right out at me. Verse 5 told me to 'not be afraid, for I am with you; I will bring your children from the east and gather you from the west. I will say to the north, "Give them up!" and to the south, "Do not hold them back." ' Then came v. 10, where it says, ' "You are my witnesses," declares the Lord, "my servant whom I have chosen." ' And when I had finished reading v. 19 I was utterly stunned.

> 'See,' said the prophet, 'I am doing a new
> thing! Now it springs up; do you not perceive
> it? I am making a way in the desert and
> streams in the wasteland. The wild animals
> honour me, the jackals and the owls, because I
> provide water in the desert and streams in the
> wasteland, to give drink to my people, my
> chosen, the people I formed for myself that
> they may proclaim my praise.'

I put my Bible down, convinced that God had spoken to me. I phoned Simon up and read him the verses too. Weird as it seemed at the time, it was clear that God had picked a couple of divvies like us for this purpose, and that he was going to do a new thing through it. All that stuff about seeing a way in the desert and streams in the wasteland were the direct answers to the things we had been praying for. Some of those nutters we had taken on at the factory definitely fitted the 'wild animal' description, and to think that they would soon be meeting and praising God was a dream come true.

When we met with Val Grieve, he told us that the next day he was going to a meeting of the key church leaders in Manchester. He invited us along, and to help turn on the charm, Simon and I decided to turn up wearing our best suits. We later found out that we looked like a couple of drug-dealers, but the assorted vicars and pastors were kind enough not to mention it. Instead they listened to us asking for their support. We told them that if they were prepared to support us and set up some serious missions, then we would take the risk and book the Apollo Theatre for a week. These church leaders had never met us before, but to our amazement they all agreed that the idea seemed to be one of God's. With them behind us we booked the Apollo right away, wrote to all the churches and took a guy on to help us administrate the whole thing.

What followed a year later was amazing. In the run-up to the big week there were three hundred local missions, which all helped pull in over 20,000 young people to the event that we called 'The Message '88'. For seven nights we stuffed the place full of performers like Gloria Gaynor, Paul Jones and Mike Peters from The Alarm. We had loads of Christians bands who were hip at the time, like Heartbeat, Triumph and a couple of lads in a pop combo that called itself Except for Access.

So many good things happened, but at the end of it we were exhausted. We had spent a year working on it, and we were shocked to find out that someone had declared braces uncool again. Simon and I both knew that the business needed lots of work put into it, especially as we had started The Message with a budget of about £60,000, but as time had gone by and more opportunities and expenses came along, the budget had gone up to £100,000. God had brought all of it in wonderfully, apart from about £6,000. As the business had slowed down, this was not good news, and we spent three months trying to sort things out. The Apollo were understandably starting to get a bit stressed about their cash, but our overdraft was at the maximum and that six grand seemed like a long way off. As I sat in our office in Longsight, I asked God what was going on. If I was sure that God was in it before, now the event had been and gone I was absolutely positive; so many good things had come out of it that the whole thing had God's signature plastered all over it. There had been plenty of people saved and loads of ministries had sprung up. How could it be that we were skint and in debt to the venue? I asked God to step in one more time and provide the cash, but driving home that night I felt tired and low. The phone rang as soon as I walked through the door.

'Hello,' said the voice at the other end of the line. 'I'm an 87-year-old lady and I would like to give you some money.'

I can remember thinking that I was a 28-year-old man who would certainly like to get my hands on some of her money. She told me how she had invested in an investment package that had gone bad. Along with many others she had lost all her savings, and it had been years before she got any back. By this time she had told God that since she had no need for it, she would let him have it. She then told me that she planned on putting a cheque for £3,000 in the post that night. To say this encouraged me was an understatement, and as she told me where she lived I went round straight away with a bunch of flowers. As well as being polite, somewhere in the back of my mind was the hope that she might give me the cheque there and then.

Walking into her house was like walking into the presence of God. She was an awesome old lady, another Olive Clarke, and as we started to pray together she put on her head covering and cried out passionately to God for the young people of Manchester. My cunning plan had a double pay-off: not only did she give me the cheque that night, but she gave more than she said, making it out for £4,000. I hoped it wasn't a mistake and paid it in as soon as the bank opened the next day.

Within hours we had another surprise. A VAT return arrived in the post, and we suddenly had enough money to settle up all the accounts for The Message '88. It was as if God had said that he was behind it all, but that he wanted us to learn to have faith and to believe that when he calls us to do something then he will provide. That has pretty much been the story of our last ten years; God has stepped in with some wild provisions, but so often it seems that he leaves it till the last minute. We have never had much money in the bank, but every time that we have taken a risk on something that we have believed God was into, he has always provided.

It seems to me that there is a link that exists between ministries of vision and small bank balances. I know loads of people who are fired up with big ideas about things they can do for God, but who have very little cash. People of vision, people of passion who want to see things get done simply cannot stand to sit on loads of money. I know when I look at £1,000 I like to think that I don't see security, I see a wage for someone working in the inner city. In my experience, churches who live off their interest are nearly always dying out. From the start we've always tried to be a ministry that lives on the edge. That means that when it comes to virtually every pay-day I'm asking God when the money's going to appear. Each time God turns up. Over the years our budgets have increased, but God has always been incredibly faithful.

Getting back to the story, after the close call of The Message '88 Simon and I decided to get seriously stuck into our business. Some of the church leaders had other ideas, and they came to see us to talk about putting on The Christmas Message '89. They felt like things were on a roll, and that to stop now would be foolish. So, nervously, we agreed. We took on another person to travel around the churches to get them fired up about putting on missions. As the missions happened throughout the year the sense of excitement mounted. At the same time things got steadily worse for the business. On the morning of 21 December 1989 Simon and I sat in the liquidator's office, signing away our business that had finally gone bust. Later that evening I was preaching the gospel to nearly 3,000 young people at the Manchester Apollo. It was a confusing day. I remember asking God what was going on. I had tried to be a good boy, I'd tried to be faithful and do the mission for him, yet there I was with a bankrupt business on my hands. I spent sleepless nights asking God, Why? I couldn't see why we had ended up with all this debt and aggravation when all we had been were two faithful, hardworking boys. It just didn't add up.

Then I learnt a lesson. If you think of it as a coin, then God's provision has a flip-side. In the midst of the euphoria of my youth – the falling in love and getting married, seeing the business grow and watching all the exciting things that were happening around me – I had missed out on this valuable lesson. Christianity isn't a cop-out, it isn't a bypass of life's problems; Christians do have businesses that go bust, they do get cancer, they do have family members that die and they will have horrible things happen to them. Sometimes God will step in and sort it out in an instant; he can heal, restore businesses and pour piles of money and orders in if he wants to. But at other times God can be the one who pulls the plug, teaching you lessons that you will only take on board once he has your full attention. What Christianity is, though, is a way through life's problems, providing everyone with the power to go through them. That Christmas God had me sat down in the classroom, making sure I learnt that lesson. I am sure that he was also giving me a new desire to go into full-time Christian work, and yet early on in 1990 Simon and I committed ourselves one last time to resurrecting the business. We were determined not to be sidetracked, but to get on with trying to sell bum bags, braces and belts and any other daft stuff we could shift. My mate Mark Pennells had other ideas.

Mark had played at one of the Apollo gigs in 1988 in the band Except for Access. Like many of us he had been amazed by the things he had seen God do at the time – he'd been working more and more in schools with his band, and he now found himself with a fresh passion for getting out there and reaching the people who needed God the most. He came to see Simon and me with an idea for something he wanted to call 'Message to Schools'.

Years later I remember sitting in a World Wide Message Tribe prayer meeting when God spoke to me through that classic verse in Romans 8 where it says, 'We know that in all things, God works for the good of those who love him' (v. 28). Right down the centuries Christians have twisted those words to mean that God will turn every situation around for good, even the tough things. For example, if a business goes bust, then there will soon be another one along that will make even more money. The theft of a Ford Escort should really be a cue for rejoicing at the imminent arrival of a brand new VW Golf. If our girlfriend comes out in a rash and dumps us, then surely it can't be long before that page-3 stunner comes bouncing round the corner. All things working together for good? Rubbish! What the Bible goes on to say in the two verses that follow is this, 'For those God foreknew he also predestined to be conformed to the likeness of his Son, so that he might be the firstborn among many brothers and sisters.'

In other words, the good that God is going to bring out of all things is that we will become more like Jesus. Like Jesus, that may mean going through some tough things, but the truth is that we cannot ignore this reality. If we want to become more like Jesus with each day that passes, we need to trust God. If we do, then even the most horrific experiences will help with the job of transforming us 'into his likeness from one degree of glory to another' (2 Corinthians 3:18, RSV). The big questions that face us all are: Are we doing that? Are we being transformed from one degree of glory into another? Are we being transformed into his likeness with ever-increasing glory? Am I more glorious as a Christian, more like Jesus today than I was yesterday? Am I far, far more glorious than I was a year ago? How much do I resemble his Son? *That*, I believe, is what God wants to do through all the trials, the problems and the difficulties of life; to shape and mould us, to put us through the fire sometimes, but only so that we can come out purer and more like his Son, who becomes easier to spot in us.

The Birth of the Music

Since leaving Huddersfield University, Mark Pennells and Zarc Porter had spent six years in a band called 'Except for Access. They had met while studying for their music degrees, and were both Christians with the big aim of breaking into the charts. Instead of six years of glamour, however, they went through six years of frustration as they travelled to dozens of meetings with record labels, all the time getting nowhere. Plenty of these big label people showed an interest, but after nothing happened, the boys realised that they were continually being 'bottom-drawered'; placed away for safe-keeping along with all the other acts there wasn't quite enough confidence to release. By keeping them down in the drawer at least the labels knew that they could still make a bit of cash should the band develop a bit of a buzz or happen to write a killer song. There are so many people – in fact I would say so many brilliantly talented Christian musicians – who waste their lives by chasing record deals and elusive hits. Even if they do make it, more often than not all they end up with is fifteen minutes of fame and a swift transfer to the bargain bin.

Mark and Zarc visited them all, and one time were

sitting in the offices of Bill Latham, Cliff Richard's manager. In bounced Cliff in his tennis gear and Bill introduced them by telling Cliff that here were two young lads trying to break into the music business. 'Hi,' said Cliff, 'Aren't we all!' before running off for his game of tennis.

That seemed to be the story of those years, endless visits but no success. They were a good band and did some good gigs. They tried to be evangelistic, and often I would be preaching with them as they did it, but there was a general sense that too much time had been wasted that could have been used otherwise. This all came to a head for Mark and Zarc during 1988 and 1989. The band had been doing more schools work (which seemed like a fantastic opportunity), plus they'd played at the two Message gigs which had seemed so credible and where so many young people were becoming Christians. Mark in particular got a real desire to evangelise. Even though he didn't feel like much of a preacher, his heart was totally up for seeing young people get to know Jesus.

As Simon and I chatted with Mark, we listened to him describing his frustration at trying to break into the secular music scene. Zarc was working nights in a garage in order to help fund the setting up of his new recording studio (Perfect Music), and Mark was absolutely skint. We weren't doing too well ourselves, but Simon and I thought that they were both talented, and we agreed to do what we could. We contacted some other businessmen and Mark chatted with some of his friends. Over the next few months between us we raised £7,000 to get Mark on the road.

Since the first time we met it had been obvious that Mark and I were going to get on well. When Simon and I agreed to help Mark and Zarc out in 1991, the two of us spent quite a bit of time together, talking through the many possibilities that lay ahead. We both agreed on schools as the main focus for Mark's work, and soon began to lay down some basic principles that might help keep us on the straight and narrow. We thought we were setting up a project that might run for a couple of years; we never guessed that it would last for so long and grow so big. Still, the principles must have worked, and they've been at the heart of everything we've done ever since.

The first principle that we knew we had to adopt was the belief that Manchester would be our primary focus. There were enough young people in the area to keep us going for a lifetime, and besides, Mark had had quite enough of travelling all over the country doing gigs he couldn't stand, being fed nothing but cold quiche and vol-au-vents.

The second principle that I wanted to put in place was the word of God; we wanted the Bible to be at the heart of everything. From the start Mark and I agreed to spend more time preaching and teaching the Bible than doing the pop tunes that Mark was going to sing. As before, this was something different, and we knew that if we didn't get things sorted at the start, we would both end up working on something neither of us was totally happy with.

Finally we decided that we should never lose sight of the fact that it was young non-Christians that we were working for. This went hand in hand with the decision to make Manchester our priority, and we had seen too many churches pour valuable resources into misplaced projects. A staggering amount of the church's energy goes on the fat and healthy flock who are already saved and have no need of evangelistic messages. Those people are saved and are going to heaven, so the church needs to get a different set of priorities. From the very beginning we made it clear that it was the lost who would be receiving the bulk of our resources.

Looking back on it now, those principles have served us well. Sticking to a diet of Manchester, the Bible and the lost might not be the most exciting way of living, but keeping it simple has made it easier to avoid distractions.

There was one final principle we put in place back then which has served us well throughout our history. Having talked for ages with Mark about the way things often went wrong for other bands, we decided that all money earned through the band – the royalties for songwriting, radio play and all the rest – would be ploughed straight back into the ministry. This didn't mean that we would try and starve people; instead we opted for paying people wages. From then on we decided that no one would ever get rich out of the Tribe no matter how successful we became. The wages are set by the trustees, and these days the principle has been extended to include speaking fees and book royalties. Keeping our sticky little fingers away from the cash has meant that God has been entirely free to bless the work – something which he seems to have been doing with frightening regularity.

Once we had hammered out these standards we were ready for our launch. A guy called Baz Gascoigne came down to preach at a service held at Mark's church in Cheadle Hulme. Midway through he pulled Mark up the front and gave him a prophecy.

'Mark,' he said, 'I really believe God is on this thing, and that you are going to be used not only in Manchester but also in Britain, in Europe and the rest of the world. God is going to use you beyond your wildest dreams.'

After so much time spent working out that we *weren't* going to get distracted by plans to leave Manchester, this one came as a bit of a shock. The church didn't exactly have a reputation for big-time prophecies, and Mark wasn't too impressed with this latest revelation. Still, as we have found out over time, God and Baz were right.

We decided not to worry too much about the future, and instead got on with the job of doing some schools work. We started in Cheadle Hulme, and did two secondary schools back to back. During the week Mark was involved in assemblies and lunch-time meetings, while I tried to get away from the business as much as possible to join him. At the end of it all we put on a concert at Cheadle Hulme High School, in their largest assembly hall. On the night about seventy-five bored-looking kids turned up, spacing themselves out around the edges to make it look like there were even fewer of them. While they looked bored, Mark and I looked petrified, seriously convinced that we were about to kick off our ministry with a massive flop. Eventually Mark got out there and did his funky tunes and I did my preaching, after which we invited anyone who was interested in receiving Jesus to go into the changing room at the school. Mark and I sat there waiting, hoping that we might score a result and get one or two walking through the door. Within minutes we were surrounded by thirty-nine of them, all hungry for God. Mark and I looked at each other in total amazement, both thinking that it felt like we had hit upon God's agenda. To have so many people respond at the end seemed like God's way of saying that he liked the cocktail of Manchester/Bible/lost. It was, to say the least, exciting.

Mark was writing his own material for the schools gigs, and was in the process of recording a tape of his pop tracks at the little studio that Zarc was setting up in his one-bedroomed flat down the road. By the summer of 1992 the rave scene was massive and all over the country were new bands and illegal parties. Zarc's studio was soon home to more dance-orientated sounds, and I used to love sitting in on their sessions. One day I booked some time in the studio to put some rap tracks down, despite the fact that I had never been a rapper or any kind of a musician. I thought it would be a bit of fun, and Mark and Zarc liked what came out. After that I began supporting Mark at gigs, doing two or three songs before he came on.

One day I was in the studio when Mark and Zarc were playing around with a harder type of music that Mark could work with. I had been reading a book about the Scottish Hebridean revival and I started telling them about it all. What had happened in 1949 was that a guy called Duncan Campbell had been summoned to preach on the island of Lewis by two old ladies, Peggy and Elizabeth Smith. One of them was eighty-three, and the other was eighty-seven, and one had arthritis while the other was blind. They were devastated by the way things had changed on the island after World War II: where the churches had been full, they were now spewing out young people at an alarming rate. God was being replaced by alcohol. Peggy and Elizabeth were so moved by this that they cried out to God and called Duncan Campbell to preach the gospel to the island's pagan young people.

Campbell had arrived and was attending regular prayer meetings with the dwindling church membership. One night, at three in the morning, their prayers were interrupted by the building shaking from the total chaos that was occurring outside the church. People were running out into the streets, repenting. Speaking later, Campbell said that in the days that followed it was hard to find anyone who wasn't seeking God. When I read those words I was so fired up that I couldn't stop talking about it. As I finished telling them in the studio, immediately Zarc started putting some tracks down, suggesting that we write a song about it. So, within half an hour we had come up with 'Revival'; the result of our first time of working together.

We used this track in the live set, with me coming back for a guest slot after I had done my little support slot. The kids totally flipped, and again, it felt like we had really hit on something. The numbers at the gigs shot up and Mark's pop tape was hijacked by all these mad 'dancey' ideas. I had a bit of input, although it was limited to a few lyrics and ideas for songs and plenty of vocal encouragement to put more funny noises in. I liked those funny noises, and it was a great time of inspiration where we felt like we were discovering a new platform for the gospel. It was over that summer that we decided to form a band, not just to have Mark doing his solo pop thing.

The inspiration for the band's name came from some other names that were around at the time. It seemed that every other rave act had the words 'Massive' or 'Tribe' in their name, and Simon and I had just finished embroidering some T-shirts that said 'Massive Global Technics Posse'. So I suggested that we call ourselves the 'Massive World Wide Message Tribe'. Most of my good ideas seem to get a little better once Mark and Zarc have watered them down, so we ditched the 'Massive' part.

We found a singer called Elaine Hanley, who was fairly well known on the Manchester gospel scene. We also got another girl in to dance and sing with us. Lorraine Williams was a Salvation Army girl who had worked with Mark a few times before. Mark and I made the mistake of inviting Lorraine for a drink at our favourite pub and ordering a couple of pints. We were halfway though them when we realised that as a member of the Salvation Army she would have signed 'the pledge', and was sitting looking worried, quietly sipping her lemonade. Her joining the band was therefore a bit of a miracle.

It was about this time that Mark and Zarc dubbed me 'Heavyfoot'. I wasn't too keen, but I saw their point; every time I recorded a rap I used to get all excited and stamp my foot on the floor. It annoyed the neighbours so much that I ended up with a cushion underneath my foot. No matter how many times I explained it to my mum, though, she never quite got it, and worried it was something to do with wearing ill-fitting shoes as a child.

When we finally got around to releasing our first schools tape we all agreed not to put a lot of work into promoting it. *Take a Long Hike with the Chosen Few* had taken months to record, and getting out on the road would have taken us away from our Manchester schools, so we decided to sell it only in schools. There was another reason why we couldn't go out on big promotional trips, and that was because we had filled the diary with bookings for schools missions for nearly a whole year in advance. Something had happened, and without too much difficulty we were fully booked.

As we visited each school – taking assemblies, lessons and finishing off with a concert – we developed better relationships with the local churches. Over time we began to see a theme that was common to many of them: they were up for seeing God move and impact a generation, but they didn't all have the resources to disciple them. It was terrible to think of all these young kids getting a taste of Jesus, only to forget about it as all the other pressures of life overwhelmed their baby faith. It was after a couple of years of these missions that we were able to provide some follow-up material which we hoped would help. *Get God – the Video* was our first attempt. It was basic and cheap – made up of me mouthing off to the camera in a church hall in Cheadle – but it helped the churches hang on to their new recruits for a bit longer.

With *Take a Long Hike with the Chosen Few* recorded, we were putting all our energies into the missions, having almost forgotten about promoting the tape. Meanwhile, a guy called Steve Nixon, a DJ in Stoke, somehow got hold of a copy of the tape and wrote to us. He told us how he had recently been to see the

Shamen in concert. At the time their gigs were almost like evangelistic New Age services, complete with a preacher and all sorts of stuff. The idea of the potential influence they could have really disturbed Steve, and he prayed that God would raise up an answer to the Shamen – a Christian band to reach the dance-music culture. It was the very next day that our tape landed on his doorstep. From then on he seemed to go on a one-man promotional campaign. We couldn't pay him, but he just felt fired up to spread the word about the band wherever he could. He sent it to his friend, a Christian producer in America called Scott Blackwell, who owned a label called N Soul. In Britain a buzz also started to develop, with more and more orders coming in for *Take a Long Hike* . . . Scott Blackwell heard it and contacted us, saying that he wanted to release it in the USA. He paid us a bit of money to add a few new tracks and, in 1993, our first CD hit the shops in America.

Meanwhile, back in Britain the word was travelling about these mad schools workers who never left Manchester. At first we were turning down little church gigs, with fifty or sixty kids, but the more the news spread, the bigger the gig offers became. For a while people called us 'the band you couldn't book' as we literally turned down anything that wasn't in front of Manchester school kids. Soon, we decided that this didn't necessarily have to be the case, and we started to spread our wings in the summer and Easter holidays. The priorities remained the same, but the opportunities to raise extra support were too good to be missed. Even to this day, each year begins with us booking up about twenty-five missions and making

The very first Salvation Army missionaries to India, c. 1885.

Mrs Olive Clarke, shortly before acquiring her gigantic
mansion and extensive gardens.

Two cool Christian bands with extraordinary haircuts and 'tashes: (1) The Bill Mason band, 1978. From left to right: Dave Rawding, Bill Mason, Simon Hawthorne and Iain Beeston.

(2) Except For Access, 1986. Zarc Porter (left) and Mark Pennells.

Our first, and rather unfortunate, attempt at a
publicity shoot, summer 1992. From left to right:
me, Zarc Porter and Mark Pennells.

The World Wide Message Tribe Mark 1, 1995. From left to
right: Elaine Hanley, Mark Pennells, Sani and me.

The Tribe Mark 2, 1997. From left to right: Elaine Hanley, me, Mark Pennells, Beth Vickers (soon to be Redman) and, in front, Cameron Dante.

Lovely Manchester schoolies. They're what it's all about.

Giving it large at a Tribe gig – without any hair, 1997.

At Sheffield Arena, 1997.

The Tribe Mark 3, summer 1997. Back row: Emma Owen, Claire Prosser and Tim Owen; middle: Deronda Lewis, Colette Smethurst, me and Elaine Hanley; front: Cameron Dante.

With Mark Smethurst in Wythenshawe, spring 1999.

With Mike Pilavachi and Frank Green at the launch of Soul
Survivor – The Message 2000 in Salford, October 1998.

Preaching at a Message 2000 bash.

With Michele, Sam and Beth, summer 1999.

The Tribe 2000. Things have obviously
gone well to pot since I left!

sure that they are prepared and followed up well. If there are any gaps left over then we fill them with whatever opportunities come along.

It was in the summers of 1993 and 1994 that we did our first gigs outside Manchester. We did a few Christian festivals – a couple with the word 'cross' in their names (although that wasn't one of our founding principles) – and played in front of our first large groups of Christians. The 1993 gig at Crossrhythms seemed to go well, but it wasn't until the two that followed in the next summer that things took off. At one of the gigs in Liverpool, Gerald Coates was speaking, and I remember trying to get him to say something nice about our ministry so we could print it in our literature. Gerald meanwhile wasn't really taking much notice of my suggestion; instead he was homing in on Mark. Just before our biggest gig so far he told Mark that the next seven years would be very important in his life. He said that he thought God was going to use Mark way beyond his wildest dreams, and that God was on him and the ministry. Mark was understandably blown away by this, but we didn't have to wait long for some sort of confirmation, as the crowd seemed to love the gig, and mobbed the stall later, buying up loads of copies of *Take a Long Hike* . . . While we knew the stuff went down well with our Manchester school kids, the nice Christians in the UK might have reacted differently. Thankfully they didn't, and things moved on.

As we got over the gig, we had a call from one of the promoters of a large Christian music festival in Holland called FLEVO. One of their main acts had dropped out, and with three days to go, they needed to come up with a band that the 10,000-strong crowd would be into, as well as all the other people who would be watching it on national television. We were probably the least qualified band in the world to do this, but they sounded desperate so we gave it a go. We turned up looking like a particularly scraggy bunch of schools workers, and stared in amazement at the set-up. The stage was huge, the lighting rig looked like it would need half the national grid to power it and the video wall was straight out of the next century.

By the time we were due on stage we had stopped staring and got down to the business of being seriously worried; FLEVO was a pretty standard Christian rock festival, and we churned out pretty non-standard Christian dance music. It could have all gone so wrong, but in the end, it all went right. They had had enough of listening to older people tell them how dance music was of the devil, and how one 5-minute dose of S-express was enough to damn your soul for all eternity. They were absolutely gagging for it. We attended a press conference afterwards where, for the first time ever, we were talked of as 'pop stars' and even 'musicians'. Both sounded funny at the time, but if you are not careful, no matter how focused you are, that stuff can turn your head. It was a lot of fun, but in some ways it was good to get back to Manchester and into the schools, remembering what we were all about.

It was around this time that we had our first approach from a UK record label. We met up with Dave Bruce, the A and R man from Alliance Music. They were interested in releasing *Take a Long Hike* . . . in the UK, or at least they were until we explained our vision and how we wouldn't be able to do anything during term-time. He went away to think about it and wrote back shortly afterwards saying that they liked the stuff but that because of our restrictions they couldn't see how it could work out. We still have the letter somewhere, and pull it out whenever we want to make them feel bad. Today Alliance are our record company, but only after some strange things happened. First, once Scott Blackwell had released the CD in America and the rest of his N Soul material was doing well, Alliance started distributing most of his releases over here. They ended up putting out *Take a Long Hike* . . . on Alliance over here and despite the fact that we were hardly ever able to go out and promote it, it sold well enough for them to sign us anyway.

While this talk of transatlantic record deals and decent sales sound nice, I was struggling about work. I could not decide whether to go full time with the band or not. I was spending all of my spare time doing ministry stuff – going out with the Tribe, being one of the trustees (we had finally become a charitable trust) and working on the wider vision for the band – yet I also had a commitment to Simon. In many ways he was the brains behind the business and I was the mouth, the one who went out on the road to get the sales and bring in the orders. There were now a lot of mouths to feed, and it was all getting to be a bit of a struggle.

The strain showed itself in funny ways at first. I am well known for getting people's names wrong, especially when I am stressed. On one particular occasion we were doing the last assembly of the week in front of the whole of Hattersley High School. I was supposed to thank the head of RE – a lovely Christian man called Mr Ryder – and the headteacher, Mr Leyland. Mark could see that my head was in a state, so he told me to think of Knight Rider. I went on to the platform muttering under my breath 'Knight Rider, Knight Rider, Knight Rider . . .' When it came round to my speech, I confidently blurted out, 'We'd like to say a big thank you to Mr Knight, your RE teacher.' Obviously the pupils all loved this. As they started laughing I realised my mistake, but made it worse by thanking their headmaster, Mr Hattersley.

At another school (this time safely away in Macclesfield) I was introduced to their new head of RE who, unlike their old one, was young, shapely and attractive. Again I was running late as I was introduced to this young woman who was wearing a tight top and mini skirt. For some reason, as I said, 'H-h-hello', a globule of spit shot out of my mouth and on to the end of her nose. We then had an incredibly embarrassing 5-minute conversation where neither of us would own up to the offending spittle while Mark was creased up behind the assembly-hall curtain.

But giving up on the business would mean something more serious than me having a better memory and less spit. Michele and I now had a couple of children and a 400-year-old cottage. Life was definitely busy, but we had a nice lifestyle to go with it. Along with the other trustees I had set Mark's wage some time before, and I knew that if I joined I would be on the same pay. Understandably Michele was stressed about the idea of moving from that beautiful house, especially as we thought the alternative would be a tiny two-bedroomed terrace. But it was clear that God was on our case and that he was leading both us and our family into full-time Christian work.

Before we had made up our minds though, we talked it through with our vicar, Donald Alistair. He was thrilled with the idea but said that it needed to be Michele's decision even more than mine as it was going to be a lot harder for her. She would be the one left at home while I would be charging around with all my exciting ministry stuff. This was wise advice but it also put even more pressure on Michele. However, at around the same time she got an amazing letter from Jane, a long-lost friend in Canada, who urged us to go into full-time ministry despite the fact that she knew nothing about our situation.

At the time there weren't any prophetic words or Scriptures that were coming my way, but everything seemed to point to the conclusion that God was in it and that going full time would be the right decision to make. In my experience that is what most guidance is like: God speaking through the practical. So often we get stressed about many things in life like which university we should go to, which person we should go out with or which church we should be involved in; all the time making things more complicated than they need to be. I believe that if we keep our eyes on Jesus we will know the answer to these questions, and even if they don't seem obvious, our lives will follow God's course. If you're looking for the classic verses on this you should turn to Romans 12, where Paul writes:

I urge you, brothers and sisters, in view of
God's mercy, to offer your bodies as living
sacrifices, holy and pleasing to God – this is
your spiritual act of worship. Do not conform
any longer to the pattern of this world, but be
transformed by the renewing of your mind.
Then you will be able to test and approve what
God's will is – his good, pleasing and perfect
will.

According to Paul, if we are prepared to present our
bodies as living sacrifices, to pay the price of really
committing our lives to Christ and being prepared not
to be directed by the world's standards, but to let the
Spirit renew us and our minds, then we will know what
God's will is. Guidance won't be a source of stress and
worry; instead it will become part of our trust, faith
and everyday expectations.

Another reason for changing the way I was working
was the amount of pressure I was putting on our
marriage. I was working hard in the business but even
harder with the ministry. Stupidly, I thought I was
being incredibly spiritual by being out almost every
night doing 'the ministry stuff'. There are so many
Christian workers who are no different from the
businessmen I used to know; they are full of bravado
about the outrageous number of hours they work,
being out all day and getting home knackered. While
they may be doing it under the assumption that it's all
very spiritual, the truly spiritual thing is to go home
and put your kids to bed. In fact the hardest thing for
me has been putting the Tribe down at 5.30 p.m. each
night and going home to be with my family.

As far as I'm concerned, there can be no doubt that I made the right decision back then. Not only was it right for me and my marriage, but it also turned out well for Simon's business. After a tough time at first, my leaving was the best thing that ever happened to the business. It turned out that I was its biggest overhead, and since leaving he has ended up making more money than ever, making sure that plenty of it goes to support the Message to Schools Trust. Of course there have been times when it would have been nice to have been earning a big wad in the business community, but over the last few years it has been my joy and privilege to be able to think full time about nothing else but Kingdom things. I have been able to focus all my energies on building up this ministry and working for revival among Manchester's young people. It has been the most exciting part of my whole life and I am so glad that in 1993 I was able to burn my bridges and go full time with the Message to Schools Trust.

4

From Demo to Limo

Throughout 1994 the work we did in schools developed. We began to provide the schools with a better, more complete service, and the news about what we were doing continued to spread throughout Manchester. We were also learning to look at our job not just as a series of lessons and gigs, but as a responsibility to follow up the young people themselves alongside their local churches. On top of this, things were ticking over nicely in the States, and after our first two non-schools gigs the previous summer, the requests were flying in.

But still the full-time staff only consisted of myself and Mark, joined a few months later by Rob Ruston who over the years has faithfully taken on all the jobs that I'm hopeless at – such as the admin. and technical stuff. Us two lads would go into school in the mornings, leading assemblies for the whole school, one year at a time. We would also do RE lessons with as many young people as possible, as well as lunch-time concerts whenever we could. By Friday night we would pull in the rest of the band and any friends and volunteers who were interested to help pull off an evangelistic concert. Almost always God would turn up big-time at these gigs, despite the fact that the crowd were often a bit on the lively side. It often seemed like total chaos during the music, with between one third and half the school turning up and jumping, dancing and making loads of noise. During those times I would be praying desperately. Somehow, when it came time to my preaching slot there would normally be absolute silence and a real sense of God's presence. It became quite usual to see between forty and fifty young people commit their lives to Christ on a night, and in general, those gigs felt like they had God's mark on them.

I say 'in general', for there were one or two exceptions. In some of the rougher schools there have been fights going on while I've been preaching. At least once or twice it has seemed that the vast majority of the audience were passionately snogging during my attempts to deliver the gospel. There was one terrible time when, because we couldn't do the concert in school, we held it in a local youth club. It was a weird place, the kind where kids were encouraged to draw pictures of gay parents and stick them up on the wall alongside condom adverts and pictures of topless women. The local church had been praying around every room during the day, and as we arrived it almost seemed like something had been stirred up, but the job had not quite been finished. The concert was terrible and the kids literally started a riot. At first they were running through our dressing-room, nicking all our things and fighting with each other. While one girl was having an epileptic fit, for some reason the rest of the kids were outside trying to smash the door down. Eventually the police turned up to calm it all down, but the kids started a fight with them. To put it mildly, it didn't go down as one of our better gigs. Thankfully that sort of gig has been the exception, and I'm sure that if God hadn't been so on our side it would have been a very different story. I often think that Satan must hate the work of the World Wide Message Tribe, when all these young people get to hear the gospel relevantly presented.

As the weeks passed we saw more and more people becoming Christians, and we tried to work in areas where the local churches could provide discipleship support once we had been and gone. This all sounded fine, until we realised that we were spending less time where our heart lay: the inner city. We always felt that that was our thing – the rivers in the desert and streams in the wasteland – but it was so hard to find churches in the inner city with any sort of developed youth work. In the few instances where we had been, the new Christians would only last a few months. Inevitably we found ourselves getting drawn out into the suburbs and into the domain of the lively churches.

While this was on our minds, things were hotting up in America. Scott Blackwell was working hard, first of all pushing *Take a Long Hike* and then, in 1994, getting behind our second recording, *Dance Planet.* This was a project we had been working on during the summer of 1993, and had started selling in the schools. Scott liked it and decided to release it and a couple of singles. Quickly we learnt that the American singles market was very different to our own, and that instead of being on sale for just a few weeks, it meant getting it played on the radio for as many months as possible. Although the majority of the hundreds of Christian

stations across the country churned out an extremely
cheesy and wet blend of music, there was a little room
for dance music. Scott released two tracks called
'Make it happen' and 'Short life', which have to go
down as two of the worst songs we or anyone else has
ever written. They were both kind of wimpy, but that
didn't seem to matter, as they did pretty well on the
Christian Hit Radio (CHR) chart. Scott finally got
round to releasing what we thought was a decent track
– one we had recorded in the autumn called 'I'm on
my way to Zion' – and it reached number one in the
charts. I think it was the first time a British Christian
band had ever done that, which all helped the buzz to
grow a little bit more.

Several of the big American Christian labels started
to express an interest, and we found ourselves being
approached by a variety of big men in nice suits who
all seemed to want us to use them to distribute the
next album. Warner Alliance were the Christian division of Warner Brothers, the biggest media corpora-
tion in the world. Their people came over to talk to
our people (Mark, me and Zarc) about all the possibilities they thought lay ahead. Again we gave them
the spiel about how tough Manchester school kids
came first and how travel would only be possible for a
couple of weeks each year. This didn't seem to be too
much of a hurdle for them, and in fact I got the
impression that they kind of liked it. Because of the
size (and turnover) of the American Christian scene it
can be easy for artists to go off the rails and wind up
being totally into a life of excess. Warner Alliance had
got some first-hand experience of this not long before
we met, when their main artist, the day after winning

no less than seven DOVE awards, had a very public 'fall'. His double life caught up with him and Warner could do nothing but drop him.

When we arrived and started mouthing off about how we put Manchester before money, I think Warner Alliance saw it as an opportunity to put their weight behind something they truly believed in. They even talked about distributing our *Get God* discipleship video to 10,000 youth leaders across America as well as all sorts of other great plans. This impressed us as it wasn't really going to benefit them a great deal in terms of record sales, but it would help to sell our vision for the schools of Manchester. We liked it a lot and signed up.

All these negotiations took a long time, and it was the autumn of 1995 by the time the deal was in place and we could give them any material to release. At the start of the summer we had been working frantically to finish off our third full-length album, *We Don't Get What We Deserve*. When I say 'we', it had mainly been Zarc who was held hostage in the studio for the whole of June. He emerged at the end with a fine album, but a dishevelled look that earned him the name 'Swamp Thing'.

Alliance got on with the business of distributing the new album in the UK in time for the new school year in September. Their American cousins were not due to release it for a while, but they were desperate for us to go over to the States to join in the fun and help with the promotions. We were fully booked with schools missions, but managed to squeeze in one 6-day and one 4-day trip either side of a schools mission at Blessed Thomas Halford School in Altrincham. On one of these trips we visited a booksellers' convention in Los Angeles. Not knowing what to expect, Sophie (one of our new dancers) and I were surprised when we turned up to find thousands of booksellers from all over the world gathering together to sell anything and everything. It's scary to walk round and see everything from Christian clothing, Christian nick-nacks and Christian albums to Jesus dolls, luminous crosses and Ten Commandment tea towels. If it had Jesus's name on it, it was there. There was even a famous actor walking around dressed up in full Superman gear, but with a 'B' on his chest instead of an 'S'. He turned out to be 'Bibleman', and he wandered around the venue for four days solid shouting out random passages from the good book.

We were sat in our own little booth giving away copies of the album, when Sophie whispered in my ear 'I just wonder if Jesus would come in here and turn the tables over?' I felt the same, that there was something not quite right about much of this multi-billion-dollar machine that calls itself the American Christian industry. Somewhere along the road it had moved well away from the Carpenter of Nazareth, opting for 'Bibleman' and perfect smiles. It was a distant and unrecognisable relation to the radical movement that is Christianity.

This set the tone for us, and there has always been a tension between this gigantic industry and our own beliefs about God. That doesn't mean that it's been all bad, for we've been out to America a couple of times and have met some quality people. Certainly there are some Christian bands that are made up of good lads who wanted to sing for Jesus, yet time and again they seem to have been sucked into this huge Christian machine. It makes me sad to see them spending ten months of the year touring from big Christian gig to big Christian gig, being cooped up on a tour bus with virtually no fellowship outside the band. There are some who, to be honest, have lost the plot, who don't know why they are doing it any more but have to keep on singing about Jesus to sell the units.

America is a strange place. As the biggest Christian country in the world there is a Christian version of everything you can think of (Christian midwives, Christian mechanics, even Christian dog trainers). It scares me that America produces 90 per cent of the world's Christian resources and yet it is a country where there are frightening levels of violence, crime, immorality, suicide and family breakdown. In so many ways it has missed the point of true Christianity, but still the majority of the population call themselves Christians.

A lot of Christians seem to think that if you tithe to the church, buy your CDs and Christian books, if you call yourself a Christian, then you can relax. They think that once you've got this sussed, then your ticket to heaven is guaranteed and you don't have to worry about all that boring lifestyle stuff. Now, all of this might be a bit cheeky coming from a Brit, and I also know there is an awful lot of it going on in the church in Britain, but – and perhaps this is due to size – the problem seems to be more intense in America.

Not that we weren't tempted. While we've never had any trouble walking down the street at home, there were times in America when we would have to run to our limos to avoid getting mobbed by the mass of screaming fans chasing after us. At one festival people were even queuing up for two and a half hours to get our autographs. However, it was never too hard to resist the temptation to take all of this sort of caper seriously; we poked fun at it (we still do) and reminded ourselves of what we're all about. It's amazing how much thinking about the broken lives in Manchester brings you back down to earth when you're standing on a stage in front of 50,000 screaming Christians. What was tempting, though, was the idea that if we took just six months out from schools work we could fund the ministry for years to come. It almost seemed plausible, but when lined up against our three original principles – Manchester, the Bible and the lost – we knew that it wasn't right.

As I said earlier, there was something different about the men in suits from Warner Alliance. They were extremely godly people who understood my concerns. They were also determined to put all their weight behind *We Don't Get What We Deserve*, which they launched with a fanfare in June 1996. They hired a double-decker bus and drove around Nashville with assorted industry personnel on board, ending up at the Sherlock Holmes' Pub for fish and chips. I think they fully expected the Tribe to be the next big thing in America, to sell half a million copies and make them loads of money – looking back, I think we were half expecting it as well. We went over to perform at the few gigs we could, all of which seemed to confirm that the kids were well up for it. However, after a while it was clear that for some reason the album wasn't going to be the big success many of us had hoped for. American sales peaked at around 50,000 copies, and I think everyone was a little bit disappointed.

There wasn't much time for feeling miserable, for as soon as we arrived home we got straight back into the schools and started working on a new project. We were still scratching our heads to try and come up with ways of helping to support all the young Christians who were dotted around the Manchester area. We had an idea for a monthly meeting where people could get together for an evening of radical worship with videos, flashing lights, dancers and all the other stuff the Tribe had become known for. As well as some bangingly loud music, we also wanted to provide clear Bible teaching and a chance for the kids to meet other new Christians. As many of these kids were being fed into churches that were struggling to support them, these Planet Life services seemed like a decent idea.

We all know that the big problem facing the church in Britain is the lack of teenagers. Sadly, what few there are seem to be leaving the church faster than ever before, despite all our fine talk about revival. If we could just hold on to our teenagers, we would be back into a period of growth. But that seems easier said than done, and most of the kids that become Christians through the World Wide Message Tribe's schools missions are still going to churches where they are one of only a handful of teenagers. Planet Life was set up to bring together a few hundred of them, fire them up and send them back to their churches to keep going and keep pressing on.

We realised that a traditional worship band format wasn't really going to work for us, so Zarc got on with the job of churning out funky versions of traditional

Christian worship songs. We were also trying to write some songs of our own that could be used in the service, and ended up with enough material for a whole album. And so *Jumping in the House of God* came into being, having been recorded at Zarc's studio during August 1996. Warner Alliance got to hear it and liked it, but as they'd spent so much cash promoting *We Don't Get What We Deserve*, and had had little return for their money, the plans for the release of *Jumping* were a little less ambitious.

At the time Warner Alliance sent it out to the Christian bookshops across the country, and it automatically got sent out to every Warner Brothers employee in America, about 3,000 in all. Usually this wouldn't have been such a big deal, as due to the size of the company the complimentary box of weekly releases that landed on every employee's desk would often contain thirty or forty CDs. The week that *Jumping* came out it was the only one in the box. Instead of putting it in the bin, most of the Warner Brothers that week were listening to *Jumping in the House of God*. Among them was the boss of it all, who went wild over the track called 'The Real Thing'. He phoned up Chris Hauser, our promotions man at Warner Alliance, and told him first that it was a hit and, secondly, that it was to be put out to the mainstream immediately.

Sure enough, the guys in LA got fired up about the single and started pumping it out to mainstream radio. Several of the major stations across the country started playing it like mad, and it wasn't long before all that initial enthusiasm looked like it was going to pay off. It went top twenty in many of the singles charts across the country, and many people thought that it was going to sell a million copies. At one stage we had a phone call from one of the big guys from Warner Brothers in LA saying, in between puffs on a fat cigar, 'We are going to make you very rich men!' They even flew a few people out to Manchester especially to tell us this, as if being told it face to face would somehow make it more real.

When the time came for the single to be distributed to the shops and go on sale to the general public something went wrong. The distribution didn't quite happen the way that it needed to, and it ended up at number twenty-two in the billboard dance charts. Not that we weren't happy with this, but it wasn't quite the global domination that the suits had predicted. I'm convinced that they weren't trying to hype us up, that they genuinely believed that the single could have been a hit. Certainly our friends at the Christian label Warner Alliance had never known anything like it. There are times when I wonder whether it was God that pulled the plug on the whole thing. Perhaps the worst thing that could have happened to the Tribe at that point would have been having a massive hit and making piles of money. It would have distracted us from the need to build up a core support of faithful prayer supporters who give us a few quid a month and help us do what we do.

I got this idea from Billy Graham's autobiography. There's a passage towards the start where he was spending a lot of time fund-raising, visiting hundreds of churches in attempts to raise support. A millionaire (rumour has it that it was John Paul Getty) volunteered totally to underwrite his ministry, offering to pour in millions of dollars over the years. Billy would be freed up from time-consuming fund-raising, allowing him to concentrate solely on preaching the gospel. Billy, to his eternal credit, told the wealthy man that he couldn't take his money. Instead of solving all his problems with a simple yes, Billy knew that he had to rely on those people who give five or ten dollars each month. Yes, the money was the same, but those small and regular donations came with something else – prayer support.

In many ways I wasn't spiritual enough to turn my back on this 'The Real Thing' in the way that Billy Graham turned his back on his own cash incentive. There was never any question that we would have used all money to spread the gospel, but it could have distracted us from building that prayer support. It is so important that a ministry is based on a firm foundation of the prayers of faithful people. If our prayer supporters found out that we were making millions of pounds from selling records all over the world who could blame them from giving their £5, £10, or £20 a month to other ministries who need it more than we would?

So the chance of having a major hit came and went. In hindsight I'm glad that it did. I don't think the World Wide Message Tribe will ever become a million-selling outfit. Instead of making a fortune, I think we will sell just enough. About 25 per cent of our income as a ministry comes from the World Wide Message Tribe, and the rest comes from those faithful, committed prayer supporters who give to us every month. That is our financial DNA, and we need to remember that as the ministry grows, the core of our support is those people who give faithfully.

As the word continued to spread around the world we started to get bigger gig offers, which became increasingly difficult to turn down. One year we were invited to the DOVE awards – the American Christian music awards in Nashville – and Warner Alliance were trying to set things up so that we could present one of the awards. As over 70 million people watch it on TV, it's kind of a big deal, and so it was with great delight that I told the men in suits that the Tribe couldn't present an award as we would be working in Ramsbottom High School for the week. Maybe there was a kind of inverted snobbery at work, but we loved turning down these massive gigs all over the world. Compared to getting stuck into a secondary school, gigs in football stadiums and TV appearances were no competition.

We can't have offended too many people as the next year (1998) we were invited back. As we weren't in school at the time, Elaine Hanley (one of our singers) and myself popped over for a few days. Instead of presenting an award this time around, we were faced with the even more frightening prospect of being nominated for a couple of awards ourselves. As if that wasn't enough, two film crews came along with us – one from the BBC filming an *Everyman* documentary and one from a Christian programme called *Alpha Zone*.

As we waited during the ceremony it was strange to think that no British band had ever won a DOVE before, and that if we didn't win, it was going to be totally embarrassing with the TV crews there. Thankfully, we won them both: Best Dance Album and Best Dance Single. After the ceremony Elaine and I went backstage for a press conference with the awaiting media. Receiving the awards had been one of the most nerve-wracking occasions in my life, and my adrenaline was pumping. I was trying to work out what to say to the media, and from what I had heard, the standard thing was to say lots of 'thank yous'. That seemed like a bit of a waste and I thought it would be better if I just said what was on my heart. So I did a little preach. I told them that I had met some great people since I had been in America, but I had also met a lot of people who had lost the plot. There were loads who had been called to be evangelists just like the World Wide Message Tribe but who had got sucked in to the whole Christian music scene. I told them that I thought there were loads who had lost it, and how good I thought it would be if they would get a passion for the lost, get fired up to get out there instead of being happily sucked into this bubble of money, fame and adulation.

I think people were quite surprised. A few minutes later I was queuing up to go into more media things and Elaine and I were holding our two DOVE awards each, when Toby from DC Talk came up behind us. He's a good lad, but Americans aren't great at getting the irony in our sense of humour. DC Talk usually win an armful of these awards, but this year they hadn't released any material and had only picked up one, so as Toby walked up behind us I turned round and started singing, *à la* Old Trafford, Stretford end, '2:1, 2:1, 2:1!' Toby looked worried, and quietly asked me if I was all right and still managing not to let things go to my head. My heart sank as he really hadn't got the joke. I couldn't bring myself to explain so I just went red and kept my mouth shut.

Anyone who knows anything about pop music, particularly the type of music that the Tribe are into, will know that it's a young man's game. In 1995, not long after things started to really take off, I was almost 35. I've never seen myself as a rapper or musician, and at the time I started to become increasingly aware of the need for somebody to come into the band and take my place quickly. I had taken on the role of fronting the band and doing the preaching but, as the ministry was growing and we were taking on more people, there were so many demands on my time to try and keep things on track. Mark, Zarc and I met, and decided to pray that God would give us a killer front man, not just somebody who could rap, sing and dance, but somebody who could preach as well. I firmly believe that God went out and saved the best possible person for that job. His name was Cameron Dante.

5

The Real Thing

As you can imagine, Cameron Dante didn't start life with such a glamorous name. He was born in Salford, one of Manchester's toughest areas, and by the time he got to secondary school he was well into sniffing glue and lighter fluid, spending large parts of his day getting high and hanging out with his Salford scally mates. Sometimes they got a bit creative, practising their home-tattooing techniques on each other. Cameron's chest and arms bear a couple of choice tattoos (his old name is written in 3-inch-high letters across his chest, and MAGIC MUSHROOMS appears down his arm).

He got into breakdancing at the age of thirteen and started a troop with Howard and Jason, who later on went on to become two of the quieter members of Take That. They practised for up to four hours each day, six days a week. Eventually they became UK breakdancing champions and came third in the world championships. At the same time as these successes throughout his school years, Cameron was working his way through the drugs on offer in the city. As so often happens, he went from sniffing glue and lighter fluid to amphetamines, cocaine and even on to heroin.

When he was seventeen he headed off to Benidorm with £80 in his pocket. By the time he got to Calais he'd spent most of his cash, leaving himself with £20 to get across Europe. Being a bit of a resourceful young man, Cam made his way down the Continent by a combination of petty thieving and hitch-hiking. Once he had arrived at Benidorm he headed for the clubs to do what he did best, and make his living breakdancing.

Having been at it for about three months, things changed when the club's DJ was sacked. Cam was offered the slot and despite the fact that he had never done it before, it didn't take him long to master the decks and work out how to hype up the crowd. He was in his element; the club absolutely rocked and over the next three years he grew to become a pretty well-known DJ in Benidorm, Ibiza and Madrid, making a nice living for himself.

The success wasn't always such a good thing, though. One day the rival club from the other side of the street decided that they wanted Cam for themselves. They offered it to him nicely (more money, more drugs), and when he refused, they sent a couple of bouncers over who tied him to a chair and threw him into a swimming pool. All he remembers is thinking that he was going to die and crying out for his mum.

As he got more and more into the club scene Cameron took more and more drugs, resulting in a fairly hazy 3-year period. It all came to an end when he was walking down a street in Benidorm and a woman he'd known for years in Salford – the mother of a mate of his – walked past him. He ran up to her saying,

'Look, look it's me, Cameron', but she didn't even recognise him. He knew the lifestyle was beginning to catch up with him so decided that it was time to come back to Manchester. He came back via Birmingham, where he made a living selling drugs and DJ-ing, before he landed a job as a resident DJ in one of the biggest nightclubs in Manchester.

Out in Madrid he'd met some guys who were forming a band called Bizarre Inc, and once he was back in Britain he got in touch and started going out with one of the dancers. Having heard him rap, the band asked if he fancied joining them on their forthcoming tour. Their first single ('Playing with Knives') was starting to be a hit in the clubs, and when it was followed up with another track called 'I'm Gonna Get You', the band were launched big-time. It got to number three in the charts and was followed up with several more hits in Britain. Then 'I'm Gonna Get You' hit it in the States, and for a year the band really did have it made. They travelled everywhere first class and had as many limos, as much money and as many drugs and girls as they wanted. Cam lived the wild pop-star lifestyle, but at the end of the year they brought out a single called 'Took My Love'. It made the top twenty, but was nowhere near as big a success as the previous single. The record company got a bit nervous and the all-important buzz seemed to desert the band.

Cam returned to England and decided to try and do some of his own stuff. Zarc knew Cameron's manager, and he was booked into Zarc's Perfect Music studio in Cheadle Hulme. Zarc happens to be one of the mildest people I know; at the time

Cam was a wild, drugged-out, profane wreck. The project he was working on was for an act called Vertigo, which was made up of Cam, another bloke and Cleo Roccus (a 1980s TV personality famous for her extensive cleavage). One of the tracks that had been chosen to launch this pop phenomenon was called 'Beneath the Sheets'. Despite this, Zarc could see something special in this lovable rogue. It was obvious that he was a brilliant rapper and dancer, but Zarc also thought he might make a good communicator. He told Mark and me, and the three of us committed ourselves to praying for him every day. We had started to talk to him about our faith, and felt for sure that a verse in 2 Corinthians 4 was appropriate. 'The god of this age has blinded the minds of unbelievers' seemed to describe what had happened to Cam. I really believe that there is a veil over the eyes of every person who isn't a Christian. That's not just for people like Cameron who were wild drug addicts, but for nice sweet people who don't know Jesus too. Prayer is the key to lifting the veil, even though it can take a long time.

We prayed hard for this to happen to Cameron and, gradually, we were sure that our prayers were being answered. First of all he started showing more of an interest in Christian things. Zarc had told him that he was a Christian but hadn't really spent a lot of time talking to him about his faith, but Cam started asking loads of questions. Then he bought a book about comparative religions. To add to our excitement, he then bought Zarc a bottle of champagne with a little tag on it saying, 'Thanks for all your spiritual encouragement'. I told him that we'd crack that bottle the day he became a Christian. He looked at me as if to say 'big chance', but the more we prayed the closer he came. Once he, Zarc and I went out for a drink and I started asking him about where he was at with God. It was obvious God was at work in his life and that it wasn't going to be long before he became a Christian.

Our Planet Life services were starting to take off, with hundreds of young people turning up to the monthly services. Zarc invited Cam along to one of them, but he hadn't been to church since he was a young Catholic lad in Salford, except to Zarc's wedding. While the service itself didn't have him repenting on his knees, he did comment to us on the way out, 'They've upped it a bit since I was a lad.' It was to his surprise and ours that he accepted one of Zarc's invites to a Planet Life service some time later. Once he had plucked up the courage to come in he found a big lighting rig, PA, video screens and all the other stuff that made sense to him.

We had a Canadian evangelist called Mike Hack speaking that night, and what he said all seemed to make sense to Cameron. When he was finished he invited anybody who wanted to become a Christian to stand up. This wasn't really the done thing at Planet Life, and in fact I had told Mike not to do it because it seemed like such a typical thing to do. For a long time the only person in the church who stood up was Cameron. He says it felt like he could hear the wind whistling through the church. To this day he doesn't know why he stood up. He says it was as if the Lord dragged him to his feet, but he really did want to give his life to Jesus. He went down the front after that service and talked to Mike, who suggested they both meet up the next day. He could see that Cameron was a guy who needed a lot of help and so he agreed to go and meet him in his nightclub the next day.

Mike Hack is an international evangelist, and he just happened to have six days left in Britain before he had to return home. He spent most of them with Cam, putting him into a spiritual incubator. Mike went down to his nightclub and read the Bible to him while he DJ-ed, surrounded by half-naked women dancing on the podiums. He went to his house and taught him the Bible, took him to church, introduced him to loads of Christians and took him round for meals at various Christian homes. He just fed him and gave him in six days the most intensive discipleship programme. It was exactly what Cameron needed.

The night Cameron gave his life to Christ I remember going back to Zarc's house and having a little party. We got the bottle of champagne, shook it up and said, 'This is the night we have been waiting and praying for . . . You're in!' I was so glad that Mike Hack took him on and gave him the time that was needed. So often we fail to invest in baby Christians, especially the ones who desperately need the support, and many don't make it all the way.

Zarc and Mark were at this point working on our latest new track, 'The Real Thing'. Cameron was so fired up and excited that he rushed off and wrote a rap about being a Christian, and recorded it double quick with Zarc for his new track. He also told his girlfriend Vicky, but she didn't quite share his sense of excitement. He had met Vicky in a gay nightclub in Manchester – they were the only two straight people in the place – and they had fallen in love and been living together for a couple of years. The trouble was that Vicky had had all sorts of problems in the past – she had suffered abuse as a child and felt that God had let her down – and the last thing she wanted was a religious boyfriend. When Cam rushed into their house and told her his news she walked out and went back home to Scotland for two weeks. But in a way, even that was God's timing, as Cameron was left in the hands of Mike Hack, and then myself and others could invest time in this baby Christian. Vicky returned and had decided that she really did love Cam, even if he was a Christian and had gone a bit weird. I wasn't too thrilled with the idea of them continuing to live together because I knew they would climb in the same double bed that they had been sleeping in over the past two years, but didn't know how to challenge Cam about it. We were teaching him things from the Bible and I felt at that time that God spoke to me and told me not to come down heavy on him and Vicky. Instead it seemed to make sense to teach them the Word and let the Holy Spirit do the rest.

We were praying that God would speak to Cam about this relationship with Vicky and in an amazing roundabout way he did. Vicky was thinking of ways to get Cam off his religious trip so one night, lying in bed, she told him that if he really was a Christian he wouldn't be sleeping with her. She thought that, when it came down to a choice between God and sex, Cam would choose sex every time. Instead he simply agreed and got out of bed, went downstairs and slept on the settee. He slept there for the next nine months until they got married.

We kept on praying, and tried to encourage Cam as

much as we could, but we also started doubling our prayers for Vicky. Cam was desperate for her to become a Christian, but it seemed like an almost impossible task; if most people have a veil over their eyes, Vicky had a double-thick duvet over hers. In many ways she hated us Christians who were involved in changing her boyfriend into a Jesus freak. One of the problems for her was that Cameron was actually a nicer bloke to have around now that he was a Christian. He was a more considerate, kinder boyfriend, and of course he had been completely delivered and healed of his drug addiction. Much as it offended her, she also had loads of people praying like mad for her. Bit by bit the double-thick duvet was lifting and, as Cameron lived the life and prayed the prayers, Vicky got more and more interested.

After about three months she agreed to go along to a 'discovering Christianity' course at the local church. They let her ask all her questions and present all her problems, and on the last day she had a real encounter with God, sensing him for the first time. We were so thrilled and were convinced that this was the moment we had all been waiting for.

The next night she went to hear me preach at a Planet Life service in Cheadle. I spoke about being hot or being cold, about being on fire for God or sacking Christianity, explaining how it wasn't enough just to be in the middle. Rather than deciding that, yes, she was going to be hot, Vicky doubted whether she really did have it in her to be sold out for God. Instead she decided that she was better off being cold. It wasn't quite the reaction I had hoped for when I prepared the message, and immediately she went back into her old lifestyle, full of clubs and drugs.

It was another five months before we could get Vicky to go to anything else remotely Christian. Cameron was pleading with her to come with us all to Spring Harvest, as by this stage he had joined the Tribe (rapping, singing and doing a little bit of speaking). Eventually she gave in, but agreed to go for only one night. It was the big Easter weekend in Manchester and the clubs were open all night. She spent the weekend off her face on drugs, but everywhere she went she seemed to be confronted by God. She met Christians whenever she left the house, and when she was at home people kept on phoning her up, talking to her about the Lord. She couldn't get away from God, and she was feeling pretty stubborn about things when she went down to Spring Harvest. They both went into a meeting where Roger Mitchell was speaking. Towards the end of the meeting, during which Cam had been praying like mad, Roger said exactly the same thing as Mike Hack had said eight months before. To Cam's amazement, Vicky stood up and gave her life to the Lord.

We were preparing for a concert in another venue at Spring Harvest. Vicky had always been very cold towards me, but as she walked into the room and gave me a massive hug, I looked at her face and could see a clear, physical transformation. The hardness had gone, replaced by a softness in her face and a joy that could mean only one thing. I jumped up on to the dressing-table and shouted, 'I can't believe it; Vicky's become a Christian!' The dressing-table snapped off the wall and collapsed with a great crack.

Later I had to crawl to the stage-manager in the hope that he wouldn't get too mad.

In so many ways Vicky has become the perfect partner for Cam. Because of all that she has been through she has a tender heart, and after having a shell of hardness and being so opposed to God, she has softened up so much. A few weeks later Cam and Vicky were baptised together in the same baptismal font during an incredible service. A week later they got married and changed their names by deed poll to Cameron and Tori Dante. Finally Cam was able to go back upstairs to his double bed, this time with his wife.

Cam's arrival was a double bonus for me. Not only did he bring to the band his wicked talents as a dancer and a rapper, but he so obviously had the heart and the gift of an evangelist right from the very start. It didn't take long to notice that when he spoke, young people wanted to listen. I committed myself to try and invest time in Cam, to teach him the Bible and help him grow. I really believed that he was the guy to fill my shoes in the Tribe, not just to front the band but also to preach.

In May 1998 I did my last concert with the Tribe, and a week later I went to the first schools mission that the Tribe were performing without me either as an evangelist or a member of the band. It was a very weird thing to watch the kids jumping up and down just as much as they usually did. Cameron came up to preach the gospel, and he preached well. When he did his appeal and invited the young people to go into class-rooms, it was the biggest response we had ever seen at a schools concert. I sat at the side of this room as the kids poured in – 106 of them – thinking that it was as if

God was saying, 'Do you really think it was ever about you?'

Since then Cameron has developed a heart and passion to become an evangelist. The most exciting thing that I've ever witnessed in my life is not just the conversion of this couple, these two people who were about as far away from God as possible, but the thousands of young people who have been affected by them. The lesson screams itself out loud from their lives: no heart is too hard to be broken into by the love of God.

6

People

By the spring of 1997 with Cameron growing like mad both as a Christian and a communicator, it became clear that it would soon be time for me to hang up my rapping boots and get on with heading up the fast-expanding ministry. We also decided that we should try to stop shuffling the line-up and get six people who we could record the next album with and who could stick together at least until summer 2000.

Cameron's arrival had a significant impact on the band and the way things worked, but over the years there have been plenty of other developments within the line-up. In fact, the decision to use the word 'tribe' in the name has turned out to be kind of appropriate. Instead of being a set group of people who make up the band from beginning to end, the Tribe is more of a collective.

When things started out there were four of us in the band: myself, Mark, Elaine Hanley and Lorraine Williams, plus of course, non-performing member Zarc. The numbers soon grew as we took on more dancers, including Zarc's wife Miriam, Collette Nuttall (who, with her husband Dave, was the first person to move into the Wythenshawe Eden project), Vicky Holt,

Sophie Woodward and Lorretta Andrews (who Mark has helped start a similar schools ministry in Milton Keynes, called Shine). In fact, the Tribe has had quite a high turnover of dancers, pushing the total up to almost twenty in five years. As you can imagine, they get worked pretty hard.

It wasn't long before we felt the need to get another wailing woman on board to help out with the singing. Eventually we came across Sani, a fantastic woman from Swaziland. Back home she had seen the country go through an incredible revival, one that was jam-packed with the most extraordinary miracles. She arrived in Manchester with all kinds of stories of a powerful move of God, especially in her own life. When she was younger, Sani's father was the king's private secretary, and he actually led the king of Swaziland to the Lord. She told us about a tradition within the land that each year the king takes a new wife for himself, who joins the others in his vast harem. The king's son set about carrying on the custom for himself once he was on the throne. He saw Sani and invited her to be his Mrs 1989, but somehow she managed to defy all the odds and get out of it. She ended up in Britain and became a member of the World Wide Message Tribe. She was an awesome singer and an amazing schools worker, yet after about eighteen months her visa ran out and she had to go back to Swaziland. Her departure left us with something of a hole.

God seems to have a knack for filling holes. Not long after Sani was back in Swaziland we met the lovely Beth Vickers. She wailed her way through a couple of years with the Tribe, after which she felt called by God to go and work for Soul Survivor. She moved down south, fell in love with their worship leader and became Mrs Matt Redman.

Shortly after Beth left, it was time for Elaine Hanley and me to do our last gig as well. Mark had stopped performing a year before, choosing instead to take charge of the choreography and the show, plus starting an exciting new ministry called Kik-Start with a vision to reproduce some of the stuff that we had seen in Manchester around the country. Elaine and I were the last of the original line-up to go. For me, there was so much else to do for Message to Schools, and for Elaine, it was time to get on with looking after her new baby Nadine (although I know that as long as God gives her breath she'll always be singing for him). The farewell gig took place in front of seven thousand screaming teenagers on 8 May 1998, and I was presented with a golden boot in recognition of my talents as a foot stamper.

What the Tribe was left with was something special: a team of six who managed to keep true to the original spirit of the band at the same time as moving it on in time with the rest of the culture. Together, Cameron, Deronda, Tim, Emma, Colette and Claire were the Tribe version 2.0. Each of them brings something fresh to the band, and each has a story to tell.

Like Cameron, Deronda Lewis's testimony is pretty extraordinary. Brought up in Tulsa, Oklahoma, her mother was only fourteen when she found out she was pregnant, and before Deronda's first birthday, her mother had given birth to a second child, Deronda's little sister. Their dad was an alcoholic, and he was often violent. It was not a happy home to grow up in, and by the time she was six, Deronda was taken away from her parents and was living with her grandmother – a deeply religious woman who went to church six nights a week. Every night after church, Deronda would hear her grandmother crying out in prayer, 'Dear Jesus, please save my babies, don't let them go to hell.' But all this seemed to do was turn her off God, and she chose instead to have a go at enjoying herself with her friends.

When she was sixteen her grandmother gave her a choice; either she could carry on living with her, or she could go back to what was left of her parents' home. They were two extremes, with the strict rules of her grandmother at one end, and the complete freedom of her mother at the other. Deronda went for what she thought was the best option, and moved back to be with her mum, settling down into a life of constant partying and entertainment. Her life was suddenly different, and of course she thought she was really living.

Deronda started dating a boy from one of the area's big drug-pushing families, getting sucked into the accompanying lifestyle. She remembers watching in horror when her boyfriend's brother was killed next to her in a drive-by shooting. All kinds of crazy things were going on, and by the time she was seventeen she was pregnant. At eighteen she was arrested and put in jail for stealing from a store where she'd worked. The store management were keen to throw the book at her and her lawyer warned her that she could be looking at as many as ten years in jail. Deronda lay terrified in the prison cell, as all the other women were taunting and teasing her. She refused to cry, but begged God to get her out of there and save her from jail. At the trial the next day the judge let her go with a warning that if he ever saw her again she would be spending a very long time behind bars. She returned to her boyfriend and for six months struggled to live as a Christian.

It wasn't until she moved to New York to try and make a break that God really got hold of her. She pulled into a petrol station just outside the city and the attendant asked her if she was new in town, suggesting that she go along with him to church. This meeting seemed to set the tone for Deronda, and for the next few days it was as if everyone she met and everywhere she went, she encountered nothing but Christians. She went to church and found it wasn't the sombre religious thing she experienced at home, but that the place was full of funky, vibrant people who were sold out to Jesus. With the help of the church she finally started to grow as a Christian, and has spent the last twenty years singing with some of the gospel greats in America, from Al Green to Carlton Pearson.

We came across her in one of those funny, round-about, God ways. We were looking for a singer after Beth had decided she was going to move on to Soul Survivor, and we met a band called Raze. Both Raze and the Tribe were both performing at a festival in America, and I was completely blown away by Donni, their awesome singer. Perhaps it was slightly naughty of me, but I mentioned to Donni that if ever things didn't work out with her and Raze that she should get in touch.

'Well,' said Donni, 'I'm happy with Raze but my mum could be interested.'

'Your mum?' I thought she was joking, and was just

about to explain the difference between us and Johnny Mathis when she started telling us what a great gospel singer her mother was.

We prayed about it, phoned Deronda up and brought her over to Manchester, having only heard one of her demo tapes. She turned out to be the most scarily godly, laid-back grandmother you could ever meet. She looks about twenty-five but is actually forty years old and full of the Holy Spirit. We all agreed that she was the one for the job, and if ever we needed proof, it came when we saw how powerfully her singing and testimony moves people in schools.

They might not have come quite as far as Deronda, but Tim and Emma Owen have also been vital to the development of the Tribe into what it is today. Tim was with the band RE:Fresh for a couple of years in Bristol and Emma was a police officer when they fell in love in London. She had a nasty accident and actually was pensioned off from the police with a bad back. In true God-like style, Emma got healed sufficiently so that she could strut her stuff for the Tribe. Tim and Emma auditioned for the band, and we were all totally excited about them. I phoned up their church leaders to suss out what they thought about them joining us, and unfortunately they were really worried about it. They felt with them getting married, and Emma having gone through the trauma of her accident at the police, that changing jobs and moving area would all be too much for them. I was worried too, but the more we prayed about it, the more peaceful and the more right it seemed to be.

I'm glad to say that Tim and Emma moved up to Manchester in May 1997, and that things did work out well. Emma particularly is a magnet for young people and we often see lots of little girls at concerts dressed up exactly like her with their baggy pants, plaits and goggles. Emma's the one who gets more letters than anybody in the office, often asking all kinds of questions. She is the kind of girl who has been through all sorts of stuff as a teenager; rebelling and turning away from God as well as struggling with an eating disorder. There are so many people we meet who can relate to what she's been through, and from her position now of being well on fire for Jesus, Emma is able to help out with loads of people.

Colette Smethurst joined shortly before Tim and Emma, getting on board as a dancer and a schools worker. While it may come as a surprise, Colette is actually the unofficial leader of the Tribe. She organises the schools missions, and keeps things together, doing far more than she originally signed up for. This is all due to the fact that Colette is the original hide-your-light-under-a-bushel person. It was ages before we realised that she had a fantastic voice, and she has ended up singing on our albums and leading worship at Planet Life. She has also shown plenty of skill as an administrator, and is just an all-round sickeningly talented woman. Yet despite all this she often doesn't enjoy performing with the World Wide Message Tribe. Her heart is really into small group discipleship, and she was one of the first people to live in the inner city with Eden. Within a few months of moving in there she fell in love with the team leader, Mark Smethurst, and they got married. Even now she often has to drag herself on to stage to leap around and grin at all the masses at World Wide Message Tribe concerts.

Colette, like Emma, also struggled with an eating disorder when she was younger. They both still suffer occasionally with their self-esteem, and it amazes me that two women who are so obviously beautiful and talented could believe the devil when he tells them they are naff.

I was at a Planet Life service recently and Emma and Colette were dancing and Dawn Reynolds (another all-round gorgeous and gifted girl) was speaking. She mentioned that, as a teenager, she had felt really bad about herself and became bulimic. I thought to myself what a bore the devil is, lying to all these girls, telling them they are useless in the pathetic hope they will believe him and waste their lives.

Girls all over the place need to learn not to believe the lies of the one the Bible calls the accuser of the brothers (and sisters!). Instead they need to believe that Jesus made each of them unique with something wonderful to show the world about God. He also thought they were so fantastic that he went all the way and gave his life for them.

Finally there's curly Claire Prosser. She's actually the woman in the office who sorts me out, running my diary, typing my letters and generally making sense of all my disorganisation. Claire didn't have a terrible background, she grew up in a nice part of Crawley with Beth Redman and landed herself a good job at the bank. Things were all going well for her when God called her into Manchester, auditioning for the band as a dancer. Gradually he's called her to live in the inner city and she lives alongside the Eden team in Wythenshawe as well as dancing with the Tribe and working at the office in Message to Schools.

With these six making the line-up for the band nice and solid, we got down to the business of recording our next album, *Heatseeker*. Of all the projects we have ever undertaken, *Heatseeker* involved the biggest struggle. This wasn't caused by a lack of ideas, it was actually a result of having too many of them. Cameron was mad about the trashing hard-core dance of Chemical Brothers and The Prodigy. Deronda is the ultimate soul diva and Tim and Emma were more on the pop tip. All I could think of saying was, 'Can't we have more of those funny noises?' It was hard work and nearly led to our producer Zarc having a nervous breakdown. The final result, we think, does have some good moments, but it sounds more like a dance-compilation CD than a band with a clear direction in mind. It was to our great surprise therefore when in Spring 1999 it won another DOVE award for us. This time no one was able to go and collect it as the heads were well and truly buried in a school in Bury.

As I write we are halfway through recording the next Tribe album, *Frantik*, and we are determined that it will have a much more homogenous sound. In many ways it feels like the most important release ever because it is not just the schools work that spins off it, but also all sorts of discipleship resources and the build-up to the big Soul Survivor–The Message bash in summer 2000.

Unlike other bands, we're not out to make music that we necessarily think is cool, we're not even out to make music that we think will sell. We like to think our eyes are blinkered and pointing solely in the direction of 14-year-old Manchester school kids; if they like it then we're happy. Recording *Frantik* has brought this home to us, and the only way that we will consider it to have been a success is if it goes down a bomb on a Friday gig in Salford.

One of the amazing things about the last few years has been that whenever we have needed somebody, God has provided. God has provided money as well as people, but if I'm honest, it's the people that really amaze me. Giving money is easy for God to do – he is, after all, the Creator and owner of the entire universe. When it comes to people, however, things get a bit more complicated. Our free will and consciousness can often get in the way of God's plans, but time and again we have been blessed with some absolutely top workers. We've worked alongside so many people with a heart for schools work, people who want to do the hard graft, to bust their gut going into schools day after day. There have been people who have come into Manchester and caught this vision for revival.

As it is a lot harder for God to find people who are prepared to lay down their lives than people who can give a few quid, I take great heart from the way the team has grown. As well as the members of the band, there are now about twenty other people working full time and another hundred or so people who volunteer. What amazes me is that we regularly get cheques in at the office from the volunteers, the guys who spend most of their spare time stewarding our concerts, selling our merchandise, rigging PA systems or loading vans late into the night. I find it hard to understand how they give so much time without getting paid and still they want to give us money. I know that God will bless them. They are the real heroes of Message to Schools and what's going on in Manchester, not the names of the band. But these secret people who counsel kids week after week, who pray like mad for us week after week, who send us £5 and £10 postal orders every week – they are the glue that holds it all together.

I get the impression that God views things slightly differently to the way that we do. We may think that it is fantastic for us to stand before thousands of screaming kids, but what really counts is time on our knees on our own before God. Add to that a desire to give sacrificially as well as holiness and all the other stuff that really hurts, and you start to get a fuller picture of what Christianity is all about. They are the things that I think we will receive an eternal reward for, and the people who are on stage must never forget that.

Discovering Eden

There have probably only been three occasions in my life when I have been sure that God has spoken to me big-style. On each of these, it has been so obviously him that I have had no other option than to get on with what he has told me to do. This first happened when I was a teenager, and I sat in a church listening to my brother's testimony, suddenly convinced that I had to do all I could to get back to God. The second time was when we started the Message. I was in bed reading through the book of Isaiah, and as I made my way through chapter 43, the 'rivers in the desert' and the 'streams in the wasteland' seemed to have been written especially for the work we were about to start. The most recent occasion was the time that we had come up with the idea for a project called 'Eden'.

The Tribe had been getting on with schools work for about four years, during which time we had always tried to concentrate on the rougher areas. Somehow it made sense to be wanting to target the places that had the least, but our work was taking us in (literally) the opposite direction. Instead of the inner-city estates we were spending much of our time in the suburbs. In these wealthy areas the churches had many more resources and were a lot better equipped to hang on to the new Christians that appeared after our week-long missions. This was the problem: when we did missions in the inner city, just as many young people responded and they seemed to be just as up for God despite all their problems, yet there was very little for them to get stuck into. Without the Christians living around them it was no wonder that they struggled to keep going.

The church has simply not been cutting it with those people. We have failed to understand quite what it is like to live on such an estate. We have quaint ideas about these people who we label 'working class', yet as many as 75 per cent of the residents are totally reliant on the state. The church has stayed away for the last 100 years, leaving the problems to fester and sending a message to the people that it does not care for them at all.

But this doesn't seem to be God's way. Whenever there has been a mighty move of God, it has always been the inner cities that have come to life as the poor get a healthy dose of the good news. This happened alongside the work of great men like William Booth, Wesley, Whitefield and Spurgeon. Whether it was Welsh miners or people from the city slums, for once it was the poor who got the biggest portion.

This has always made sense to us and so when it became clear that we were spending most of our time in the suburbs we weren't too comfortable with the idea. I booked up a couple of schools missions in early 1996 in Wythenshawe, one of the biggest council estates in Europe. The schools were keen, but as we looked around for local churches to support the missions we had a bit more trouble. We ended up working with a little church called King's Church which, when we had first met, had a congregation totalling fourteen adults and six children. The pastor of the church, a man named Adrian Nottingham, had been living in Wythenshawe for eleven years, and virtually every day he walked around the streets calling (quietly) out to God to do something about the terrible state the place was in. We're not just talking about poor street lighting and broken windows here, but a huge pick-'n'-mix of the worst social problems associated with inner-city life. Things were so rough that Adrian even felt too scared to prayer-walk around the area known as Benchill. This was the most notorious part of the estate, the bit known for drive-by shootings, prostitution and chronic drug abuse. Adrian ended up prayer-driving around Benchill, and when I saw it for the first time myself, I knew exactly why he didn't want to get out of the car.

The two schools missions we had booked up on the estate were put on back-to-back, with a joint concert at the end held in the local forum centre. Both had gone really well, but the run-up to the concert was pretty chaotic. Elaine was ill and couldn't make it, Beth was desperately trying to learn her parts just minutes before the concert began and Cameron was rushing off straight away afterwards to go skiing with Tori. Somehow we didn't have all the equipment that we needed, yet 700 teenagers turned up, and after I preached about 100 of them responded.

What was even more awesome was that they all turned up for church on the following Sunday. King's Church put on a special evening service and the congregation rose from 20 to 120 over night. Suddenly the church was full of these Wythenshawe scallies, many of whom were really up for God. It was so exciting, and seemed like the direct fulfilling of God's promise about 'rivers in the desert'. Sadly, over the next few months we heard that most of those young people had drifted away from God. To this day there are probably only six of them left in the church. While we're all pleased that their lives have been radically changed, it is impossible not to feel sad for the other 94.

The girls in the Tribe were particularly moved by these two weeks in schools. In their spare time they returned as often as they could, meeting the kids in their homes in an attempt to help the church disciple them. We found that something had happened to each of us, and couldn't shake the area from our minds. Finally we had seen both how much these areas really needed God, and also just how capable he was of changing their lives. It was obvious why many of the baby faiths never made it through the first couple of months, and no one would expect each member of King's Church (children included) to be able to pastor five of these scallies.

I met with my friend Frank Green, and talked with him about what we could do about it all. We came up with a mad idea of giving their church the dream ticket for youth work. If we were a small church, we wondered, what would we need to be able to cope with one hundred new Christians? As well as piles of resources and prayer support, we guessed we would probably need forty devoted youth workers, not just any youth workers but people who were really fired up about it. We would need a full-time team of four to go around the schools and streets in the area, as well as to have the Tribe as evangelists whenever necessary. It all sounded like the workings of a deranged mind, but we visited Adrian and offered it to him anyway.

A couple of weeks later, after Adrian had said that he was into the idea, we went to see the church leaders in Manchester. It was the same group that Simon and I had been to see ten years before when we had told them about The Message '88. This time around, Simon and I told them how we thought that God might be calling us to set up something new in Wythenshawe, that we wanted to call Eden. We asked them to give their best people to work as missionaries in the area, while we did all we could to make things happen. To our delight, they didn't just say that they would; they were madly enthusiastic about it all, and prayed for us till we left the meeting really fired up.

As Simon and I sat in the car park in Manchester talking about the meeting, a guy knocked on the window. He said that he had a word from God for us, so Simon (being more spiritual than I, who thought he was obviously a nutter) told him to get in. The guy climbed in the back of the car and said, 'I don't know if you are Christians or if you understand this sort of thing, but I really believe that God just spoke to me as I sat there eating my sandwiches. He told me to read these verses to you.' With that he started reading to us from Psalm 37: 5–11. We sat there with our chins on the floor, listening as he read the words:

Commit your way to the Lord; trust in him and
he will do this: He will make your
righteousness shine like the dawn, the justice
of your cause like the noonday sun. Be still
before the Lord and wait patiently for him; do
not fret when people succeed in their ways,
when they carry out their wicked schemes.
Refrain from anger and turn from wrath; do
not fret – it leads only to evil. For those who
are evil will be cut off, but those who hope in
the Lord will inherit the land. A little while,
and the wicked will be no more; though you
look for them, they will not be found. But the
meek will inherit the land and enjoy great
peace.

I have since found that the guy who gave us those
words is an awesome man of God who spends about
four hours a day praying and hanging out with the
Almighty. It was like God was saying, 'Yes, this is my
idea. I have got a heart for the poor and the lost and I
am passionate about change in the inner cities. I want
to see the strongholds of the enemy broken.' The
verses also mention opposition, of people succeeding
in their wicked ways and people carrying out schemes
against each other. We sat in the car after our guest
had left us and wondered where this might come
from. It was Simon who was right when he suggested
that even though we might see wonderful things
happen in the toughest areas, we would come up
against even tougher opposition in the church.

King's Church, which was a little independent
church, was about to become part of Covenant Min-

istries, which started out of the house church movement. They had been looking for a church to partner
them as they reached out to Wythenshawe, and Covenant Ministries seemed like the ideal choice. Eden had
not even started at this point, but I had no idea that
these links would cause such problems. It turned out
that a couple of the churches who were our key
supporters heard that we had got involved with a house
church (which was kind of true) and some members
started spreading rumours about activities that the
church was supposed to be involved in (which were
definitely untrue). A whispering campaign started that
Andy, Mark and the Tribe had got involved with a
dodgy movement and were trying to force people out
of the mainstream conservative evangelical churches
and into their work in Wythenshawe.

It was just unbelievable; not only were the rumours
false, but they started to have an affect on other
supporters as well. All sorts of people were pulling
their support and some were doing more than their
fair share to spread the 'news'. One leader in particular seemed intent on sticking the knife in good and
hard, and started phoning everybody he knew to tell
them to remove their support of the Tribe. It was
painful, to say the least. It was extraordinary that all we
were trying to do was get on with what we were called
to do – reach and keep young people and work with
God's family across the city – but some members of
God's family were too busy trying to undermine our
work. Thankfully we were still half-stunned from the
powerful way that God had spoken to us about Eden,
as well as the fact that the partnership with King's
Church seemed to be so obviously from God. Cove-

nant Ministries had put all their administration and prayer support behind the project and we simply knew that we had to see it through. If we hadn't been so sure about God's calling, we would have sacked the whole thing long before.

So often this seems to be the pattern that gets followed, as the devil gets us from within, killing new things at birth. The devil must have hated the idea of these inner-city strongholds coming to life, and as we saw it as an attack, we moved on with even more determination. We wrote to all the churches in Manchester, explaining things from our side, and launched the idea of recruiting people at the 1997 Soul Survivor summer festival.

As people at home slowly came back around to the idea of supporting Eden, there were more encouragements to come at Soul Survivor. On the afternoon that I was due to introduce the idea to the festival, I was talking to Phil Wall from the Salvation Army missions team. I had been telling Phil about how I was going to invite people to pack up and move to Wynthenshawe, to get their hands dirty and not take the soft option. We wanted between thirty and forty Christians to move in and make a huge impact on the lives of the local kids. That evening, just before I went up to speak, Phil grabbed me and told me how he believed that God was going to give us a Gideon's army, 300 people for the inner city of Manchester. I had never thought of getting that many people, and I went on to the stage hugely excited and preached my heart out, challenging the young people to move into Manchester.

Hundreds of them volunteered, and out of them thirty moved into Wythenshawe over the next few months. Soon we started pumping young people into King's Church and bit by bit the church started to grow, as young people started coming to faith. We haven't seen full-blown revival yet in Wythenshawe but the atmosphere there has totally changed, no question about it. I believed that it was right to strike the rock, to move people into the toughest place, so the first twenty moved into Benchill. The atmosphere there is undeniably different, and while there is still violence and vandalism, it is no way nearly as intense. Bit by bit God's kingdom is coming to Manchester, and within a year King's Church had grown by about four or five times. Not only that, but there was phenomenal growth going on in both the Planet Life meetings and local school Christian Unions. The Eden team was soon having contact with hundreds of kids right across Wythenshawe, by working in schools and hanging out on the streets. Finally we began to get a glimpse of how it all could work: not only did King's Church grow, but the other churches right across the estate started to catch the vibe.

Of course any team needs a leader, and Eden was no exception. Because it was something we were so keen on, and because we thought it could well end up being one of the toughest jobs ever, we had fairly fixed ideas about what sort of person we were looking for to take it on. Obviously they would need to have had plenty of experience working as a leader or a manager and would certainly be well into their twenties. Some sort of background of working with young people in an inner-city environment would also be up there on the list of requirements. We started talking with loads of people who we thought fitted neatly into the 'key youth leader' box, some who approached us and some who we approached ourselves. These chats yielded nothing; either we had reservations about them or they didn't fancy taking it on. Many had families to consider, and for some of them the thought of bringing up their children in one of the toughest estates in Britain was, to put it mildly, not very appealing. We fully understood, but were still left in the awkward situation of our most ambitious project so far being without a leader.

As we talked and prayed about it all, one name cropped up more than most. Mark Smethurst was a 19-year-old lad who had been among the first wave of project workers to move into the area. Like the others he was to work during the week and spend evenings and weekends hanging out with the locals and clearing up the glass after the almost daily attempts to steal his car. Despite his age and lack of 'key youth leader' status, we started to think that he could be the ideal man for the job. He was flexible, keen to learn and able to cope with discouragements, of which there would be many. Within a few weeks of him joining us on the project he accepted the job of leading it, and has turned out to be one of our very best workers.

Through Mark God gave us another technicolour example of how he loves to turn things upside down. While we were busy looking for someone with kudos and publicly recognised track record, he was waving the answer right under our noses. Who else but God would have suggested putting a 19-year-old in charge of thirty people all working in a pressure-cooker environment? It seemed foolish, but it was also brilliant, and totally in line with the way God works. He loves to turn things on their head; like getting a scruffy bunch of young Christians involved in breathing some life back into schools and downbeat areas or choosing screw-ups like you and me to spend the rest of eternity with him in heaven.

As soon as it was clear that Eden was working in Wythenshawe I started wondering whether we could reproduce it across Manchester. Could this be an answer to the problems of so many of the other spiritual wastelands? Could it be that eventually there would be so many Eden projects going on that the Tribe only ever did missions alongside them? An idea slowly emerged, crazy as all the others, but just as exciting. We wanted to set up ten Eden projects across Manchester, and with thirty working in each one, it really would be a Gideon's army. I called a meeting in Birmingham with some friends from various key youth organisations, and asked if they had the resources to put into Manchester, and if they had the desire to work in partnership. Youth for Christ and Salvation Army missions both said yes, they did believe that God was speaking to them. And so the three organisations spent the first half of 1999 sorting out the fine details and recruiting workers together.

I also met with Lawrence Singlehurst, the main man at YWAM, who also writes about cell church and has a real heart to disciple inner-city kids. I asked if he knew of anyone who had experience of discipling large numbers of young people like those who were starting to come through Eden. Lawrence's comment was 'Well, William Booth did it', and neither of us could think of anyone since who had seen big-time break-through with inner-city young people. The truth is that there are lots of faithful youth workers in the inner city, but no one is seeing the breakthrough that we are working for in Manchester. If all the mission activity that we are planning over the next few years comes off, then we are going to need hundreds of people moving in, and thousands supporting it in prayer. What we also need is a strategy for dealing with a changing culture and making sure that the commitments are made for life.

As far as I'm concerned, praying for Eden is like praying for nothing else. It feels as though, as you pray for the inner-city poor and the lost, you touch on God's heart. Jesus was incredibly hard with religious people and yet incredibly gentle with the worst of sinners. He was often accused of hanging out with tax collectors and sinners, but his answer was always, 'It is not the healthy who need a doctor but the sick.' I believe that it is time for the church to start focusing its energies, its efforts and its prayers on the sick. It's time to watch God bring those rivers into the desert. For many that will mean more than just praying and giving, but moving in long term and changing the course of their life. This is same spirit in which Robert Hawthorne moved 100 years ago. His was a one-way ticket for the gospel, for the lost. I honestly believe that there is nothing more important that I have been involved in than Eden. If we can get it right and pull in more partners who want to do similar things right across Britain, the implications are massive. Perhaps, just as things spread out from one tiny church in Wythenshawe, things could spread out from our one small corner of England and start to have an impact on the whole nation.

8

God's Ambush

As someone who has spent all of his Christian life in the Anglican Church, I have been particularly excited to see that over the last few years God hasn't given up on it. Far from trashing it, he has blessed it and used it to encourage people all over the country. His methods were typically unusual, as just when people like me were mouthing off about how the poor churches would get things going, he picked out two posh southerners to have a worldwide influence. First up was the London church with the nicest carpets in the whole country, Holy Trinity, Brompton. Their *Alpha* course (which reminds me of a confirmation course) has had a colossal impact in many different countries, introducing thousands to Jesus in a way that almost anyone can follow. What's more, this has all happened in a very short space of time. I am sure that it has God's seal of approval and, with that in place, nothing can stand in its way.

I also believe that God is blessing us all through a church right at the heart of middle-class England. Chorleywood used to be known as the town with the highest number of cars per household, but now the word is out about an offshoot of its youth work. Two top blokes – Mike Pilavachi and Matt Redman – head up Soul Survivor, which started in 1992. We got involved once it had been going for a few years, and I remember that on our first visit I immediately got on with Mike, a big-hearted man for Jesus. There are times when I feel like he 'wings it', and occasionally it looks like Soul Survivor is held together with sticking-plaster, but God is all over the event, the church that came out of it and all over the bearded wonder himself, Mike Pilavachi. Everything he touches turns spiritually to gold. That's the kind of person I want to partner. God's favour is resting on Soul Survivor and it is clear that Matt Redman's worship songs have blessed the church like nobody else's in the last few years.

It was on our first visit to the festival that I spent a bit of time with Mike. We found that God was saying the same thing to our two ministries – that combining young people with a radical relationship with Jesus is a recipe for huge change. Being one of those people who go out of their way to encourage the things they believe in, over the years Mike gave us more and more room at the events to get our message heard. When we had the idea for Eden Mike wanted us to use the event in any way that we could to help launch the project. We had an incredible intercession afternoon when all the seminars were closed and thousands of young people got together just to pray for Manchester and Eden. Mike gave me a preaching slot on the main stage, and everywhere he went he was talking about Eden and the work of the World Wide Message Tribe in Manchester – needless to say, I liked the guy.

We were both at Spring Harvest together in 1997, the Tribe were leading the youth venue and Mike was doing something with the older ones. He and I went for a coffee with Matt Redman and Cameron, and sat around half-expecting it to be one of those chats where we did a bit of networking, had a laugh and compared stories of feeling too old for youth work. God, it appeared, had other plans. He ambushed our cosy chat and changed everything.

We started talking about Manchester, Eden and some of the things that were going on at the time. I was telling them about my dreams for a big mission in the city, and explaining how we were already sensing that Manchester was ripe for a large-scale move of God. The year before Mike had put us in touch with a German guy called Roland Werner, who was organising a city-wide mission in Dresden called 'Christival'. It was an event that had exploded and grown beyond their wildest dreams. Having started out praying for 10,000 to come along, they ended up getting 35,000 Christians, and even had to turn 20,000 away. There were thirteen venues across the city, all rammed full with a variety of evangelistic events. The idea was that the Christians spent the afternoons out on the streets, witnessing and bringing people along to the evening meetings. Literally hundreds were becoming Christians each day, and for one week Dresden was taken over by the gospel. There were helium balloons on the corner of every street saying 'Come follow Jesus', and posters all over the city invited people along to the evening events. The Tribe had been doing a few gigs and none of us who went had ever seen anything like it. Chatting with Mike,

Cam and Matt, I started going on about how wonderful it would be if we could do something like that in Manchester, getting thousands of Christians on board to really blitz the city.

A few days later Mike phoned me up. I could tell that he was excited by the way he was shouting and not letting me get a word in. Slowly I managed to piece together what he was saying; he had a mad idea to cancel the Soul Survivor festival for the year 2000. Instead of having it in the usual field in Somerset he wanted to move it and the 20,000 punters up to Manchester for two five-day missions. In the morning they could meet for Soul Survivor-style worship, teaching and ministry in the Holy Spirit, and in the afternoons they could get out on to the streets and start meeting people to bring along to the venues for evening events across the city. Of course this took my breath away, and any plans for a mission I had previously been working on were blown out of the water. I'd been thinking about the possibility of hiring the Manchester Arena for one or two nights in the year 2000, but Mike was suggesting booking not just that venue, but every other place available for ten nights running.

I realised that through Soul Survivor's resources we could do this. We had a meeting and started to talk about how we worked on The Message '88, laying the foundation of getting support from the local churches. Back then we had 300 churches behind us, and were sure that we could do it again. We suggested that we would be able to set up an office and spend two years working on 'the ramp-up'; building support and making sure that the biggest youth mission ever attempted in the UK would have plenty of churches ready to pastor the influx of new Christians.

Without really realising what the implications would be and just how complicated it could all get, we both agreed to go for it, and publicly work together. We started pulling in partners; Youth for Christ to look after all the street work for the big event, Oasis to take on board the social action work. We wanted social action to be right at the heart of this thing, and we wanted to present a holistic gospel; not just to beat people over the head with a Bible, but to meet their real needs. We decided that 60 per cent of the delegates should be working on up-front evangelistic work and 40 per cent should be involved in social action right across the city. Quickly plans began to develop; we could establish and maintain some sort of a homeless project, we could paint hundreds of houses on the estates and clean up neglected areas.

At Soul Survivor 1997 Mike announced the plans which were greeted with a standing ovation. The whole festival was buzzing about Soul Survivor–The Message 2000. It was fantastic to see so many people who were up for it, and to think that so many young Christians would be coming over to Manchester for the mission. It was like the wildest dream slowly becoming a reality, and at times it seemed too good to be true.

Returning from the summer festivals we knew that we couldn't leave Soul Survivor holding the baby. It was our city, in that we were based there and had the initial contacts, so we got on with the business of setting up the office and recruiting a team. The local churches were our main targets and we had learnt a fair bit about working alongside them from the previous six years. We had found out how vital it was that the churches we wanted to support us were given plenty of training, resources and opportunities to get involved with missions. They also had to be allowed to learn from their own mistakes and add their own unique flavouring to the events. From the start, Soul Survivor–The Message 2000 has been seen not as a stand-alone event, but as a climax of a whole year that is stuffed full of missions and outreaches. Throughout the twelve months that lead up to the event there will be over 500 local missions going on and over 100 social action projects being identified and prepared for. This way, when the thousands of workers arrive much of the city will be ripe; they will be able to work at the heart of the city's problems and people that commit their lives to Jesus will have loads of support for them over the months and years that follow.

Mike Breen, a vicar from Sheffield, recently told me how he believes people will write about these events in centuries to come and describe them as a big move of God. Living with it day by day it often doesn't feel like much of a move of God. Sometimes the work we do feels more like throwing mud against a wall, seeing a few people become Christians and seeing life break out slowly. But the church in Manchester is not the same as it was when I first became a Christian. The prayer movement in this city is significant, and the amount of people coming to faith, their fire and passion should be enough to convince anyone that something is going on. We want to milk that for Jesus's glory, we want to see a city turned around. We don't just want to see a few people come to faith, we want Soul Survivor–The Message 2000 to be a significant move of God, not for the glory of these two organisations but for the glory of Jesus, the only one who deserves it.

Tied in with this dream that seems to be becoming a reality is an even crazier idea. If we can do this in Manchester, drawing in people from all over the world to see what we have done, maybe they will want to do it in their cities. While we get on with following up and keeping all the young people who will come to faith perhaps others will target big cities worldwide for something similar. Could it be that the pattern of a year of local church mission and activity, prayer and preparation that culminates in thousands upon thousands of Christians getting stuck into an intense mission would work elsewhere? If it could, and if people were committed to targeting the toughest and poorest areas, then just imagine the impact they could have. That's what Soul Survivor–The Message 2000 is all about; us trying to fulfil our calling to see every young person in Manchester being given repeated opportunities to accept or reject Jesus. That is precisely what we're about, and it is that goal that we will continue to chase, heads down, until we can put our hands on our hearts and say that it has happened.

One of the best decisions we made in the early years was to spend one day each month away from the schools and the offices. This wasn't an excuse to bunk off, but a chance to spend valuable time praying and checking with God that we were keeping on the right track. We have always wanted to do our best to fulfil the calling that he has for us and have known for a long time that prayer is a vital part of making sure that it happens.

These have consistently been great times, and through them I have developed a theory on prayer. I'm convinced that it takes time to really hear from God. Often when we start praying we are so weighed down by excess baggage and surrounded by so much cack that it takes more than a few minutes to really break through and touch the heart of God.

Prayer can often seem like wading through mud. For ages it can seem like God's on holiday and that nothing can bring him back. But suddenly all that can change, and you find yourself right in there hearing from God and receiving direction. We've been through this loads of times, and it's definitely been the case that most of our good ideas have started during the times of revelation that follow the hard slog.

We had one particularly memorable day early on in 1997. My friend Frank Green was praying for me when God powerfully touched me and knocked me right off my feet. I was left on the floor feeling decidedly un-Anglican, when a clear picture came into my mind. It was of a circular saw spinning at great speed. As I looked, I could see logs falling into a basket by the side. I felt as though God was saying, 'It's good what you've been doing with the Message, and you've actually been cutting through a bit but it's been hard work. Pretty soon my power is going to kick in and the whole thing is going to speed up to such an extent that no one could ever say it was through human efforts.' I honestly believe that is what Soul Survivor–The Message 2000 is all about – an unprecedented opportunity to take a huge leap towards our goal.

9

The Power of the Partnership

There doesn't seem to be any way of writing this without it sounding dodgy, but over the years, I've met some amazing women. I'm not alone in this either, as William Booth (yes, Mr Salvation Army) was famous for saying, 'Some of my best men are women!' I'm not entirely sure of the exact qualities that so impressed Mr Booth, but I know for sure that through a handful of inspiring women I have learnt many valuable lessons. Over time I have come to see that Christians – both as individuals and as groups – tend to succeed or fail on one specific point: partnership. As groups we move between the two extremes of unity or destruction. As individuals we face a choice between living life for ourselves or chasing after God with all we've got. Partnership is the key to success; if we sort it out things will move on.

In 1997 we went to South Africa to help Tearfund make a training video called *Desire*. As part of the trip we visited a township called Pietermaritzburg, and there I met an Indian nun who was living in the middle of one of the most violent parts of the world. In the area thousands of people have died from tribal warfare, and it remains the most intimidating place I have ever visited. Yet this old, poor nun chose to live in a minute shack with no running water and the threat of violence all around. Kids in rags were running in and out of her house and she literally glowed with love for Jesus. At the back of her home was a small chapel where people could come in, and she would give them communion and pray for them. The prayer time we had in there was totally inspiring, and we all were in awe of this remarkable woman.

I asked her what her ministry was, looking for the secret technique she had used to gain the respect and love of the locals. 'Just to be' was her reply. It turned out that she had never leafleted the area, she never put on any gigs and she wasn't trying to be an evangelist. She simply was there, hanging out and giving her time and energy to whoever was in need. She made it a better place to live by being a radiant Christian in a very dark place, and despite the fact that she was softly spoken and about four feet tall, she made this loud-mouthed Manchester evangelist feel very, very small.

I remember meeting another woman from a totally different culture, whose background couldn't be further removed from that of the Indian nun in Pietermaritzburg. Baroness Caroline Cox, a 62-year-old grandmother, is the deputy speaker in the House of Lords, and a woman who could so easily opt for living the high life. Instead she chooses to spend large parts of her life flying in rickety planes into the most dangerous parts of the world. She exposes torture and persecution, and brings to the world's attention the plight of Christians in countries such as Sudan, Burma and Afghanistan. Again, she is a wonderful woman who has a dramatic effect on the world around her by choosing to go against the flow.

If you phone up our offices there's every chance your call will be answered by another pretty amazing young woman. Alex is our poorly paid part-time secretary, who is also one of the Eden volunteers. She didn't let us know until quite a while after she had joined us, but Alex is actually heir to a 50-bedroomed castle in Scotland. She has grown up as a member of the aristocracy but has chosen to live in Wythenshawe in a council house for Jesus.

They are the kind of people who have understood just what it means to be a Christian. They are all excited about being in partnership with God, and are prepared to make the sacrifice that is part of the deal. While your calling may not be to live in a township in South Africa, the inner city of Manchester or to fly off around the world and risk your life exposing persecution, God wants you all the same. He wants us to discover for ourselves how great (and tough) it is to be in partnership with him. Somebody cleverer than me worked out what this actually meant, and suggested that God has no hands but our hands, no feet but our feet and no mouth but our mouths. He was right as well, for without us on board Christianity struggles for workers.

Stuck above my desk at the moment are my favourite verses from Ephesians 3:20–1 where Paul says: 'Now to him who is able to do immeasurably more than all we ask or imagine, according to his power that is at work within us, to him be glory in the church and in Christ Jesus throughout all generations, for ever and ever!'

Those verses are about partnership, about God (who is able to do immeasurably more than all we can ask or imagine) being at work in us. I know that I can ask some pretty amazing things of God, and I can imagine some even more widely exciting things that I might be too embarrassed to share with people, but God can do far more than anything that I might be able to come up with. And how does he do these things? The good news is that it is not just by his power, but by his power in us, his partnership with us. To be in partnership with the living God is a seriously good privilege, especially as it means getting used to doing big, eternal things. I believe that God wants people to get excited by the potential to be used by him and start to make a difference. So what if the difference that you're going to make doesn't turn out to be the most public or noteworthy, we are all called to make a difference, to do our bit. From his perspective, God sees how all our efforts fit together, and he knows just how many anonymous works it takes to change a nation.

The evangelist J John recently pointed out that one snowflake can so easily melt on your cheek, but enough snowflakes together can stop traffic. That gives me hope that we can change the course of Britain, as long as we all get involved.

Apparently Mother Teresa was once approached by a cynical journalist who asked whether she really thought that her work could have an effect on poverty worldwide. Mother Teresa wisely replied that what she was doing may well be just a drop in the ocean, but that the ocean is made up of many drops. If we don't find our own place in God's incredible tapestry, we will miss out not only on a whole load of personal experiences and blessings, but we will do nothing to help prevent the rot that threatens to drag down even more lives than it has already. That God chooses to use dummies like us is a sure sign that he values these partnerships and longs to work through them even more. I believe that we are going to see increasing numbers of young people doing their bit and working together with God and each other. They are a generation who are growing up sick and tired of the disunity and lack of passion in the church, and with their radical commitment, the rewards could be massive.

A book landed on my doorstep a couple of weeks ago which detailed reports from around the world of amazing revivals that have been happening. I read through the chapters on Pensacola and Toronto, and was shocked to see a chapter about Manchester and our work. Deep in my heart I know that what's going on through us and around the city is a long way off from being considered fully blown revival. Yes, good things are happening, churches are coming to life and young people are coming to faith, but revival? We may be seeing things that we haven't seen for a long time in the church in Manchester, and all the signs are there, that if God sees fit, he could bring a massive move of his Spirit in this city; there is so much more to come. Thankfully the levels of excitement about the future are higher than I've ever experienced in my twenty years of being a Christian. There is a unity among the churches that for years and years was sadly lacking, but we must not let it go to our heads.

Eric Delve is an evangelist who has travelled all over

the world preaching the gospel. He recently said at the Evangelists' Conference that Manchester was the hardest place he has ever done mission. I had heard that Moody or one of the other great evangelists once had to cancel a mission in Manchester just because the churches were so disunited. While he was desperate for a little support to help him get out and preach, the local churches were busy arguing about who was going to introduce the evangelist and who was going to organise the committees. Churches are now starting to work together. So there is expectancy, there is unity as well as prayer. The prayer network pulls in 700 or 800 Christians each quarter to get on their knees before God. Their denominational backgrounds may be different, but their aim is the same; to get things going again in the city. Sir Fred Catherwood is president of the Evangelical Alliance, and on a recent visit to the network he described it as the most exciting meeting he had been to around the country, due largely to the sense of expectancy, the unity and the prayer.

The latest exciting thing that has been happening in Manchester is a new relevancy in the churches. Where once they were old, cold and half-full of Christians who wanted to get away from the world outside, now they are tailored to the people who need to hear the gospel the most. As they realise that church has to make sense to people on the street so the petty religiosity seems to get left behind.

The Anglican Church has been dosing up on some new life that has been going around it, but does that mean we should sit back and lamely wait for something exciting to come and knock on our door? What we should be doing instead is being a little more like the Reformers who shaped the church in the sixteenth century. Their motto was 'always reforming', as they pulled the church services out of Latin and into the language of the street. When Cranmer put his Church of England prayer book together it was a radical street book in a language that people could understand. It communicated to a specific generation and brought the service up to date with the rest of contemporary culture. The problem was that most of the reformers were burnt at the stake and 350 years later, many of us are still using Cranmer's book.

Clearly the Salvation Army was once the most awesome organisation, used mightily by God. But the brass bands were the music of the streets 100 years ago, the tunes they played were the dance tunes of the day, and of course they received plenty of criticism and condemnation for it. It worked back then and managed to reach thousands of people, but today the tunes just don't seem to cut it. The Salvation Army, the Anglican Church and even the movements that have only been around for thirty years or so all need to ask themselves if what they are doing is the best way of reaching the lost for Jesus. That's why I'm so thrilled that Salvation Army have got a new bunch of radicals like Phil Wall coming through. They've picked up on the Eden project, and I wonder if there's a chance that, if their Eden project takes off in Manchester, Edens everywhere could become a part of their work. Perhaps this could be a small part in turning the Salvation Army around from being the fastest declining movement to one that once again is seen as cutting it in the tough places in the inner city. The two posh southern churches I mentioned – Holy Trinity, Brompton, and Soul Survivor – are helping to perk things up in the Anglican Church, and thankfully, there are plenty of other churches and ministries queuing up to be a part of the action in other denominations. With increased expectancy, unity, prayer and relevancy we have a firm foundation for God to move in. In themselves they are no guarantee of revival – frustratingly we must leave that to God.

10

The Meaning of Life

A friend of mine recently got back from a trip to Nigeria, where he had made some amazing discoveries. We're not talking about wildlife or woodcarvings here, but concrete evidence that God is on the move big-time in Nigeria. He was invited there to speak at a night of prayer. Not too amazing, you may think, but when he turned up it soon became clear that this was no low-key affair. The prayer night was attended by a colossal one million people, all of whom were there to cry out to God from dusk till dawn. For most of the people, however, this was small-time, as several weeks before there was a prayer meeting which was reliably reported to have pulled in up to seven million people. It was the largest gathering in history, and again Jesus was the primary focus.

Understandably my mate was blown away by all this. He was also curious, and went about tracking down the two men who were right at the heart of the revival. When he finally got to chat with them, he was desperate to find out exactly what they thought it was that had got (and kept) things going. He expected the answer to be something like prayer, unity or renewed holiness. But while each of those things was evident, he was surprised to get a different answer from the men. Independently of each other, both men told him that the reason behind this powerful move of God was just one thing: testimony.

Hearing this reminded me of that bit in Revelation 12 when Satan is thrown out and a loud voice in Heaven says, 'They have overcome by the blood of the lamb and the word of their testimony.' Testimony is obviously a powerful thing, and the way that it has brought about a change in Nigeria is through people simply telling others about the good things that they have seen God do. This in turn encourages people to expect God to do something great in their lives too, and before long there has been so much gossip about the gospel that people are longing to see exactly what God is going to get up to next.

I imagine that these testimonies started with people claiming that God had healed them from a headache or provided some little thing for them. Slowly, more dramatic stories would be told, having an even greater impact on the audience. Once they got into the league of talking about how God had raised someone from the dead, then you can imagine how keen other people would be to meet up with God for themselves.

Once my mate had told me about his trip we made sure that the next Planet Life service had plenty of room for testimony. We invited anyone to get up and tell the rest of us what good things God had done for them. The stories ranged from one girl who was on her deathbed when people prayed and she was healed to friends who had fallen out and had been reunited as they came to God and became Christians. There was a buzz as people shared the good things that God had done.

In a way this book is just my attempt at a testimony. I'm well aware that there are far better bands than the World Wide Message Tribe, far bigger ministries than Message to Schools, far more spectacular miracles and faster growth happening even in Britain than we are seeing in Manchester, but God has done something and he deserves the glory. As I have come towards the end of this book, I feel as though I have really only just completed chapter 1. There is so much future, so much potential in Message to Schools and all the related projects that the story is in no way complete. The thought of Edens spreading right across the tough parts of Manchester and on to other towns and cities across the UK is one that gets me and a whole load of other people excited.

Remember all that stuff about how important partnership is to us, how we need to hook up with God and be united with each other? The Eden projects have taken a new twist of late, and are now aiming to provide a service that gets right to the heart of many of the area's problems. Alongside the team of Christians who move in and work with young people in schools, on the streets and in the church, there will be central buildings that offer practical support. These life centres will provide anything from professional counselling to drug rehabilitation, from pregnancy counselling to work on personal finances. We will be buying some houses on each estate to provide accommodation for both the short-term homeless and those who have trouble finding housing elsewhere. Each Eden project will now follow this pattern, and we hope that it will mean that we won't be just beating people over the head with a Bible, but actually meeting real needs, getting alongside people and showing them the love of Jesus through what we say and do.

There's a bloke I know called Terrence Rosalyn-Smith who used to be a particularly wealthy international banker. He's still got cash, but now he uses it to set up projects in the inner city. When we first met he told me how he was convinced that what young people need – especially the sort of damaged, dysfunctional young people we meet through the Eden projects – is to find out exactly what they are worth. He went on to explain that he felt there were three key areas in which this needed to happen. First they need to find and be aware of the fact that they have a solid community around them; secondly they need to find their value in work, and thirdly, through worship, they need to realise that there is a God who made them and loved them enough to die for them. Terrence went on to explain that he knew his part in the plan was to work, setting up small businesses in the inner city that would take on the unemployable young people. It struck him that what we were trying to do with Eden was to accomplish the second two goals – the worship and the community – so why not join up and go for all three? Something about what he said made perfect sense, and we realised that the idea had phenomenal potential. By moving the Christians in and getting them to spend time with the locals we were catering for the spiritual well-being of the young people, and by helping them get back to work as well as dealing practically with other problems they face we should have a much greater chance of seeing long-term change.

At the heart of our idea to have 300 workers getting stuck into Eden projects is a belief that we need people who will make a big statement to others by living in a way which is opposite to the spirit to the age. We want to see people who are turning their back on this incredibly materialistic world in which we live, moving out of their nice pads and into a grotty place simply because they love Jesus. It's a movement that God is all over and one that I'm glad he has promised to bless.

Today's society lives in the shadow of an enormous false god, a god that even Christians bow down and submit their lives to. The god's name is money, and not surprisingly worshipping it always ends up in bitter disappointment. We live in the most materialistic age in history, and David Watson, who I believe was an awesome man of God, had this to say about it:

> There has been a great attack on the Eastern
> church in the twentieth century. That attack is
> persecution, and it has failed miserably, you
> can't persecute the church out of existence.
> You just crush it and it comes back stronger
> than ever before, and yet the great attack on
> the Western church in the twentieth century,
> has been materialism. Materialism has been
> such a success for the enemy.

Mr Watson was right, and sadly, the church has suffered for the attacks. Materialism has managed to squeeze the life out of plenty of Christians, many of whom have honestly believed that happiness is linked to possessions. Of course, few would admit to such a vice; I mean, it seems like such an obvious trap, doesn't it? The truth is that loads of us have signed up for 'things' instead of signing up for God. It's not limited to rich people either. I know plenty of poor people who are locked into a cycle of believing that if they get the things, happiness won't be far behind. You need only watch the queues in the Wythenshawe newsagents on a Saturday night at 6.45 p.m., to see loads of desperate people buying a fistful of lottery tickets with their last fiver in an attempt to get happy. They're there each week, despite both the ultra-slim chances of them winning more than they spend as well as all the evidence that actually winning the prize jackpot often leads to unhappiness and paranoia. As George Michael summed up the dilemma in one of his early solo songs, 'What does a young boy do when all his dreams come true?' He certainly had all he ever wanted – money, sex and power – but not only was it not enough, it was actually an unpleasant situation to be in. If this book makes you think about one thing, I hope it is this: getting sucked into the race for more possessions is a waste of time. Life is not made up of acquisitions, but of inspirations – spending more time with God will make you happier than spending more cash. Of course God doesn't mind us having some things, he doesn't mind us owning nice things, but I'm sure you have heard it said before that those things can so quickly own us. Unless we 'seek first the Kingdom of God' we are not going to get all the other things that God has got stored up for us. Those things might not be possessions, but they will be all the things we really need to live a fulfilled and contented life.

So what exactly is a young boy or girl to do? I'm sure that one of the best ways of combating the powerful grip of money is to give it away. This isn't just about giving away 10 per cent and keeping the rest, but giving as a response to the incredibly extravagant love that God has poured out on us. There are many young people around who are kidding themselves by saying that when they get older they'll give money away. The trouble is that when that big wad does land up in your wallet, it's pretty hard to break the habit of keeping hold of it. I admit that it can seem foolish to be giving money away when you're struggling yourself, but there's always someone worse off than yourself, and we can always give till it hurts. Besides, whoever said that Christianity was supposed to be easy?

There are loads of Christian business people who start out with the best possible intentions, planning one day to give stacks of cash to God's work, but the day never seems to come along and sadly, God's gift of the skills of the entrepreneur aren't used to their full potential. I'm not anti entrepreneurs; in the ideal world those gifts would allow them to enjoy some of their money, but to give much of it away to help support God's work. But many of these Christian business people fall into the trap of living just beyond their means. Instead of settling for one particular house, car or holiday destination they feel the need to constantly upgrade to a better model. With all these financial pressures bearing down upon the wallet, there can be no wonder that the idea of giving a large proportion of it away seems to make so little sense.

I am convinced that God wants to raise up a new

generation of business people, those who are focused on mission and reaching people with the gospel. These money-makers will be incredibly successful at raising funds, but the priority and focus of their lives is not money for themselves or their next business venture, but cash for the Kingdom.

Jesus said these scary words in Matthew 6:19–24, and they're clear enough not to need any commentary. As I read them they always remind me of what I really am like.

> Do not store up for yourselves treasures on earth, where moth and rust destroy, and where thieves break in and steal. But store up for yourselves treasures in heaven, where moth and rust do not destroy, and where thieves do not break in and steal. For where your treasure is, there your heart will be also. The eye is the lamp of the body. If your eyes are good, your whole body will be full of light. But if your eyes are bad, your whole body will be full of darkness. If then the light within you is darkness, how great is that darkness! No-one can be a slave to two masters. Either you will hate the one and love the other, or you will be devoted to the one and despise the other. You cannot be a slave to both God and Money.

Now I'm sure that what you've been reading over the previous few pages might have upset you a little (if it has, that probably means that you're normal). There are others in the church who would probably be even more upset about it, though, especially as they consider personal wealth to be a sign of God's blessing. This 'prosperity gospel' suggests that if you give some of your wedge to the church or a particular ministry, you will receive 100 times that amount as a return blessing from God. While in some ways this is quite true – we do know that God loves to bless us – it kind of ignores the fact that those blessings come pre-packed with a whole load of persecutions and difficulties. What's more, Jesus told us to store up our treasures in heaven, rather than on the earth, and I don't think that it takes a genius to work out that BMWs probably won't be on God's list of eternal blessings in heaven. It only takes a little time to read through the Gospels and to discover that instead of being full of followers who were dripping with gold, Jesus's disciples were poor and, later, persecuted.

Few would doubt that Paul was the greatest Christian that ever lived. Towards the end of his life he was able to say (in Philippians 4), that he had known what it was to be in plenty, yet he had also known what it was to be in want. The prosperity gospel seems to sign up for the first half, and neatly ignore the second. What is more, Paul isn't only talking about cash, but about safety. Among the times when he was 'in want' were the three times when he was beaten with rods and the five times in which he received thirty-nine lashes. He was shipwrecked on three separate occasions and was in constant danger whenever he was on the move. He had struggled and toiled, he often went without sleep, and had known hunger, cold and nakedness. Paul's testimony is hardly in line with a triumphalistic prosperity gospel view, hardly a great example of the three C's (Christ, Cash and Comfort). Paul had known both sides of the coin, but the things that were most precious to him were godliness and contentment. Paul encouraged others to chase after the same goal, believing that in pursuing godliness, contentment would not be far behind. Paul didn't couple godliness with wealth or success, but with the most elusive and indefinable of blessings: happiness.

If you read Revelation 12 you come across a bit where the devil is cast down and the people of God are victorious in the name of Jesus. The passage explains that their victory over the devil comes through the blood of the lamb and by their testimony. It also points out that these believers did not love their own lives even until death. In other words, they knew their place.

That's the great need of the hour; a group of people who have got hold of the cross, who know what sacrifice is all about. For these people the realisation that God loved them enough to die for them will carry them through all manner of difficulties. We need these people to not be shy about proclaiming their faith and testifying about the good things that God has done. They need to be the sort of people whose hearts and minds are not set on possessions but on living for eternity. Like Paul, they are sure to come up against beatings, dangers and poverty, and hopefully, like him, they will be able to repeat his words from 2 Corinthians 4: 'We fix our eyes not on what is seen, but on what is unseen. For what is seen is temporary, but what is unseen is eternal.'

I was involved in my first mission a few weeks after I became a Christian. It was in Manchester in 1978, and that man David Watson was heading it up. Before we

went out on the streets one night, a guy called Will
Rogers came along to give us a pep talk. I'll never
forget what he said:

> When I die, I want to hear the trumpets
> blowing from the angels and I want to see the
> saints dancing. I want them to hear them say,
> 'Come in, Will, enter the joy of the Lord.' I
> want a massive party because I have done stuff
> for Jesus. Despite all my imperfections I want
> to have made a splash.

A few weeks after he said those words to us I walked
into the Scripture Union shop and saw a little picture
of Will Rogers. Underneath was a handwritten message that he had died a few days before, and above it
were the words 'Good and faithful servant'. I could
almost hear the champagne corks popping in heaven.

That's it, that's what life is all about. Satan doesn't
want us to realise it, but this life is just a breath, a mere
few seconds and a speck in all eternity. The only
things that will last are those that will be remembered
in heaven. Forget the cash or the labels, it's only
what's done for Jesus that matters, so let's live like it.

In 1990 my dad died after a struggle with heart
disease that lasted several years. As he lay in bed
during his final hours, fighting for breath, he asked
my mum to sing to him. She chose that slightly cheesy
old chorus, 'Turn your eyes upon Jesus'. One part of it
reads 'look full in his wonderful face and the things of
earth will grow strangely dim in the light of his glory
and grace', and as she sang the presence of God came
into the room and my dad calmed down. They spent

the rest of the night singing their way through the *Mission Praise* songbook, and in the early hours of the morning my dad sang his way out of this world and into the next.

When he died my mum saw a picture in her mind of Jesus coming into their bedroom and picking my dad up. He carried him into a beautiful garden where she heard some familiar voices. Some she recognised as belonging to his Christian friends, but one stuck out as the voice of his brother who had died the year before. As she listened, my mum heard them saying to my dad, 'Hey, George, come in. Look at this; it's wonderful here!'

11

Postscript: End Thoughts

Before I finally do get round to signing off this book, there are a couple more things I need to say. I have been praying that there will be people who read it that will want to respond to stuff that God's has been saying to them. Among you, there might be some potential Eden workers who will move long term into the inner city of Manchester. As you have read this book and maybe as you have heard about Eden in other places, you've thought that this is what you want to do with your life. You're at a point in your life where you can make a big decision, one that will mean turning your back on the materialistic culture we live in and living alongside the poor and the broken for Jesus. If that is you, if you believe that God is maybe calling you to be one of the 300 people who will move into the inner city of Manchester over the next few years, please write into our office:

The Message, PO BOX 14, Cheadle, Cheshire, SK8 2FE.

We'll send you all the information about Eden, an application pack with details about the churches we're working with, the areas we are working in, and the whole vision of Eden. We take up loads of references and spend a long time moving people through the selection process, so don't expect to be packing your bags just yet. It's a tough calling, and the vast majority of people who apply don't end up moving in, but if you believe that you could be one of the few, get in touch.

The other group of people that I want to address at the very end of this book, are the people who still aren't Christians. Why miss out any longer? If you have read this book and you've spoken to other Christians, maybe you've heard the Christian message before but still haven't responded. Responding right now would be a very good thing to do. If you're not ready for that, why not pray and ask God, if he's really there, to help you get to know him? When you've said that, read a Gospel from the Bible (I suggest either of the ones in the New Testament called Mark or John). Read it with an open mind. As you read it, I believe that God will speak to you and you will realise that Jesus was no ordinary man, but that he really was God come down to earth on an incredible rescue mission. You will find as you read it that you will get confronted by Jesus, a guy who spoke the most amazing words. In fact, those words were so amazing that in 2,000 years there has been no one who has been able to improve them. The words he spoke then are still firing people up today. Read the Gospels and you will find out that he proved it by doing the most amazing miracles. Jesus really did put his hands on blind eyes so they could see and on deaf ears so they could hear. He brought dead people back to life on a number of occasions, and even his enemies couldn't deny his extraordinary powers.

Most importantly, you will find that you are confronted by someone who loved you enough to die for you. The weird thing about Jesus is that the most important event in his life was his death. It was more important than all the times he spoke to huge crowds, and more important that all the times when he healed people. It sounds strange, but when he was on the cross he was taking the full force of God's anger for all the wrong stuff in your life. Jesus was punished for all your rotten thoughts, attitudes and actions. The Bible calls him our substitute; in other words, he came in our place. I know that I deserve to be punished for all the wrong things that I've done, but Jesus was punished in my place and that is fantastically good news. When you get hold of it, it's enough to keep you going for all eternity.

There are no special words or ceremonies to go through to become a Christian. It's simply a matter of turning away from anything that is wrong in your life, believing that Jesus is the Son of God and that on the cross he took the punishment for all that is wrong in your life and asking him to take control of your life. He will not force his way in; he is a perfect gentleman. But if you want to give him everything, if you are prepared to commit your life to Jesus today, he will come in. I know that loads of people in Manchester and all over the world find it helpful to say a little prayer in order to say yes to God, to tell him that they're really serious about it all. This is a prayer I suggest you use if you want to do just that:

Lord Jesus, I want to follow you. I know I've done loads of bad things. I know that I don't deserve to go to heaven. I'm sorry and I turn away from everything that I know is wrong in my

life. Thank you so much for dying on the cross
for me. Thank you for taking the punishment
for all the wrong things I've done. Please take
away all the rubbish in my life and fill me with
your Holy Spirit. With your help, Lord Jesus, I'll
live all out for you, for the rest of my life. Amen.

It is because Jesus really is alive that, as you pray that
prayer and mean it, he will come into your life.

After Jesus died, his body was put in a tomb and a
massive stone was rolled across the entrance. Once
again he proved that he was who he said he was, and
that he had beaten death once and for all; he came
back to life and walked around for nearly six weeks.
He was seen by hundreds of people and then went
back to heaven and sent his Holy Spirit to live inside
every real Christian to help us live the best life
possible, and to let us know we will go to heaven
when we die. The Christian life is one that is full of
sacrifice, commitment and hard work. It's also a life of
contentment and a life of power. This power is available both when we're alive, and when we're dead, as
like Jesus, we too will go to heaven one day. Jesus said
this: 'You will know me and you will know eternal life.'
He meant that if we hook up with him, he throws
eternal life into the deal. If you did pray that prayer,
please write into The Message office at the address
above and we would love to send you some literature
to help you go on with God.

PS You may have noticed that I firmly believe that
God is on the move in Britain and is raising up a whole
generation of people who are totally Mad for Jesus!

Resources available from The Message

GET GOD 2000 is the latest discipleship resource. This is a six-week introduction to the Christian faith which aims to help teenagers get stuck into the Christian faith and discover for themselves just how totally awesome Jesus really is. The six-part video (priced at £12.00) features Andy Hawthorne and The World Wide Message Tribe – and some great footage of WWMT concerts – and deals with the nitty gritty, the real basics of the Christian faith. To accompany this is the GET GOD 2000 book (priced £5.00), which is published in the popular glossy youth magazine format.

FRANTIK – THE ESSENTIAL GUIDE is a basic explanation of what a Christian is and what following Jesus really means. It's particularly aimed at young people, many of whom are not used to reading books like the Bible. The booklet is written by Andy Hawthorne and includes the text of Mark's gospel from the New International Reader's Version of the Bible – a simpler, more accessible version of the popular NIV Bible. It is designed in a full colour CD inlay format, and costs just £1.00.

The booklet is also available in a pack with a 70-

minute kick-start CD: five minutes of words and music from The World Wide Message Tribe a day, for fourteen days, that is intended to get brand new Christians hooked on God's Word and into the habit of a lifetime. The CD and booklet packet sells for just £5.00.

FRANTIK – THE ALBUM is the latest offering from The World Wide Message Tribe, designed to lift your spirits and rattle your ribcages. It's about being consumed by God, expressing more than just human feelings, overcoming your limitations by encountering the living God. The album is packed with the band's combined vocal and lyrical talents, demonstrating the breadth of talent within the Tribe, and features the debut rapping of Emma Owen. This CD costs £15.00.

Together these resources are designed to help fulfil the vision of The Message: to see a day when every young person in Manchester has had repeated opportunities to accept or reject Jesus, and every one of those who accepts Him is swiftly integrated into funky, Bible-believing churches.

For more information or to order these resources, check out our website: www.message.org.uk, or contact:

The Message
PO Box 14
CHEADLE
Cheshire
SK8 2FE

Tel: 0161 491 5400